The Law of Thirds | A Division for Thought

Simon John Lee

First published 2012

Author: Lee, Simon John.
Title: The Law of Thirds / Simon John Lee
ISBN: 978-3-033-03680-2

Copyright © 2012 Simon John Lee

All rights reserved. No part of this publication may be reproduced or transmitted in any form or by any means, electronic or mechanical, including photocopying, recording or by any information storage and retrieval system, without the prior permission in writing from the author, publisher and copyright holders.

Cover by Anya Trew and Grinko Volodymyr.
Illustrations by Rob Anderson.

To beauty & truth

Contents

Preface 7
Introduction 13
The Single-Issue Machine 15
Approaches to Thought 19
Divisive Thinking 21
The Law of Thirds 25
Two, Four to Twenty-four 31
Two 35
Four 39
Five 47
Six 51
Seven 55
Eight 61
Nine 67
Ten 71
Eleven, Twelve and MORE 75
Twenty Four 83
A Law of Thirds Interlude 87
Einstein's Theory 91
Mantras 97
Three Letter Acronyms (TLAs) 103
Currency 109
Three-Legged Stool 123
Freedom 129

Triage	133
Placebo Effect	137
Color	143
Winners	147
Traffic Lights	153
The Art of Effective Communication	159
Picture Art	167
Three Point Turn	173
Dining	179
The Johari Window	189
The Three Appeals	193
The Third Way	199
Three Represents	205
Preamble	219
The Art of Thirds	229
Necessity: The Mother of All Invention	241
Art of Management	247
Those who have not mastered the Law of Thirds	259
An Apple a Day	267
An Issue of Economic Proportions	273
The Wave Principle	277
Epilogue	281

Preface

Three, two, one - liftoff... Apollo 11 reaches into the sky, each stage depletes, disengages, discards to the ocean. History is made. Armstrong, Collins & Aldrin demonstrate 'the right stuff' and return suspended by a triplet of parachutes. Deployment of three righting bouys correct the impact to the ocean.

Three rocket stages, three men, parachutes, bouys, but why?

I nearly convinced myself that The Law of Thirds need never be written. I was quite certain there were any number of titles available to the reading public that promoted everything I wanted to talk about, but in greater detail, and with great rigor. I, like many of you I'm sure, have read a few. If you have, then you'll be familiar with the way in which most approach the subject. Many are conceptual. Some are hypothetical. Some are pie-in-the-sky.

You may well be familiar with some of the concepts illustrated in this book, though you may never have put a name to them. A fair number of people already use the techniques in their daily lives, though most often it is unintentional or an act of the unconscious mind.

When was the last time you heard something like, "We asked the scientists to suggest a name for our new product and the consensus was that a three syllable word would be most memorable." And once the name is announced, you're left chuckling at the extraordinary expense that went into ferreting out what seems such an obvious conclusion: the three syllable choice was, in fact, the correct choice.

Shakespeare himself was a master of this law, even making a joke to himself in Hamlet - when Lord Polonius asks Hamlet, "What do you read my lord?" Hamlet simply replies, "Words, words, words". - there is more to this law than just words I promise you.

This book, I hope, will provide you with the same information and thinking tools that the 'scientists' in the previous example have at their disposal; those related to and dictated by the Law of Thirds. Indeed, by reading through this book, your brain will be primed with this exceptional, yet common sense technique of thinking. It explores the natural thinking processes of our brains, and does so without bogging you down with the three most common errors of writing: too much text, too little substance, and an overabundance of high-mindedness. You won't find any of those here.

The book breaks down any number of prejudices as to what is actually 'in the mind' and in doing so, explains in a formal, yet uncomplicated manner just how the Law of Thirds can be used to your advantage. Yes, we'll experiment with any number of examples illustrating this new insight into thinking, processing, and implementing, using everything from Japanese art and Einstein's Theory of Relativity to capture the concepts. And we'll talk about men and women who get it – from Van Gogh to Tesla – and some who don't.

There are many books out there on the market that discuss thinking, yet there are remarkably few concerned with solutions. This is a book about creating solutions.

Many such books teach us only to be realistic. To work with what we have. Think, and it will happen. I, for one, think about winning the lottery. It's never happened, but it's fair to say I don't buy a ticket very often.

Constraining our thoughts to our abilities may sound like a great idea. But what if I want to run a marathon, yet have never run more than ten miles? Should I eliminate the idea because it's out of my comfort zone?

What is constrained thought exactly? I think it is best described as furnishing ideas or concepts that fit within the scope of what we feel we are capable of. That's pretty constraining, isn't it? And yes, acting within one's constrained thought might be worthy advice for those among us whose ideas or concepts tread closer to the world of fantasy than reality, but constraining our thoughts does little to facilitate the execution of an idea.

Forget constraint. Execution requires chopping the problem up, dissecting it, throwing the pieces against the wall and seeing what works. Yes, we're all familiar with such inimitable pearls of wisdom as, "Every journey starts with a single step." The problem is, after ten steps or so, the counting gets a little boring. Our minds drift off to some landmark in the distance. We find ourselves quite content to focus on this milestone while consciously or unconsciously pushing the rest of the plan to one side. A journey of three steps is all we really need.

This book will allow you to harness the skills and talents that you currently possess, to magnify them, to make them manifest, and to put them to work out in the real world, a marvel for all who encounter this cache. It will make creating solutions simpler and more effective; it will give your confidence an irreversible boost; it will give others complete confidence in you. What better gift.

Fundamentally, this book is very simple. And while complete mastery of the Law of Thirds is reserved for the very few, one does not need to be a master of the concept to help it change your life. Chapter to chapter, this book is a journey that will build your understanding of the Law of Thirds, while increasing your ability to use thought and the natural processes of the brain to become a more effective person. I urge you to read the book section by section, and then to re-read those sections that resonated most strongly with you.

For those who long for more scientific proof of the Law of Thirds and the material I present within these pages, I suggest you review the works of George Miller or Alfred Yarbus, exceptional researchers who approach their material from a far more scientific methodology than I do here. You might also try the writings of Sigmund Freud, though the chances of getting bogged down by the breadth of his research is considerable.

Be advised that science, prodding, or introspection did not determine the conclusions drawn in this book. Rather observation and correlation form the basis for this treatise. I have observed ordinary people making the best possible decisions in the blink of an eye; I have seen clever people over-analyzing and formulating outcomes that could only be described as disastrous; I have studied the most unlikely candidates using the Law of Thirds, though not always consciously, and been amazed at the remarkable results.

Yes, some people are completely aware of the power of thirds. Others use it accidentally. The goal of this book is to make you conscious of the concept and fully versed in its tools. Because once you know it, the power will be self-evident. And once you master the tools, the potential is unbounded.

Introduction

Thought is our most vital life force. We use thought throughout every day of our lives. Thoughts even manifest themselves while we sleep. One of the most natural desires of the human condition is to think. Sometimes we think too much, sometimes too little.

Each thought we have is a living thing. It manifests as an electrical current or chemical pulse in our brain. These currents or pulses can snowball, gain momentum, and lead to creativity or productivity beyond our wildest dreams. They can also fade away with little residual effect. This amazing, definitive fact makes thought both a creative force as well as a dynamic one. All that we create and produce is a manifestation of our thoughts.

Each thought has the potential to reveal any number of reactions. A thought has the ability to create panic. It can trigger the most primitive and vital responses, drawing blood from our limbs and directing it to core organs, increasing our heart rate, and driving yet more thinking. We also know that thinking is one very powerful way to take flight. It is a means to retort, to rejoin, and to respond. Thinking has the power to relax us. It can generate an atmosphere of complete acceptance.

One thing is clear: thinking is responsible for everything that is important to our lives. Above and beyond the wonders of nature, everything we see around us exists because you or I or someone else had an idea – a thought – and that idea went on to become what we see as we move through our days. From the architect who patterned the place we call home to the very glyphs that form the very words you are reading right now; these things all started out as thoughts.

It goes without saying, therefore, that thought – at its highest level – is a hugely important skill to cultivate, to nurture, and to master. When combined with other talents you may already possess – be they artistic, athletic, mathematic, entrepreneurial, psychological, or social – thought allows you to harness your gifts and to change your world, big or small, personal or professional.

This book encourages thought as an active, energizing process, providing you the reader with the three conscious tools of change:

- It will help you train your brain to become a better thinker
- It will give you a broader outlook, instilling calm
- It will offer a default or fallback way of thinking that you will find remarkably effective.

The Single-Issue Machine

Most of us would agree that computers are arguably one of man's greatest inventions. Computers are remarkable in their ability to execute instructions according to its master. Unlike people, computers cannot think.

Computers operate on procedures known as algorithms. An algorithm is a set of distinct, well-defined steps. The algorithmic approach breaks up a problem into a series of simple steps – or single issues – each of which requires little thought or effort.

The computer is, for all purposes, the quintessential 'single-issue machine'. It comes with a clear idea of what procedure should be performed, but it does not answer the questions how or why. If we look at it that way, the computer, though often extremely fast and efficient at addition and multiplication, is nonetheless also extremely stupid.

There is no thought with the single-issue machine. The single-issue machine cannot, as thought does, build character. It cannot, as thought does, serve our mental, physical, or spiritual health. It cannot be, as thought is, a catalyst for change, growth, or learning.

What happens when we allow ourselves, a human 'biological' entity, to devolve into a 'single-issue machine'? We no longer explore the how or the why. We operate more as the computer does, performing simple steps, one at a time, going through the motions, and, for want of a better term, becoming dumb as well as numb. We are, at that point, unable to think. We become ineffective.

If, at this point, we find ourselves unable to connect with the how or the why, we no longer have the ability to think outside the box. We are trapped.

When, in the course of a day or a week or a month, we tackle one issue at a time and devote the vast majority of our attention to that issue, life begins to feel like a series of crises, one calamity after another. Moreover, people viewing us from the outside see a person on the brink of the abyss, out of control, and flirting with disaster.

The single-issue machine focuses only on meeting a deadline, on performing, on an all or nothing attitude. What, we ask ourselves, becomes of living? What becomes of questioning? What becomes of inviting happiness into our lives by expanding our horizons, seeking the new and the unexplained, and challenging our perspectives?

Let's use a simple, yet telling example to explore the reasoning behind our hypothesis. Take the one-hundred-meter sprinter; an athlete built of nothing but freak physiology. What does he think during those nine-and-a-little seconds from starting gun to finish line? Surely there can be nothing? After all, the race is a most brutal demonstration of the machine that is man; putting one leg in front of the other, a skill we learn in the first year of our lives; metabolizing carbohydrates into fuel, a feature blessed of the most basic of primitive amoebic life forms. So what can thought have to do with it?

And what of tactics? Most would say that a sprint hardly ranks with chess when it comes to tactics, that the sprinter races only against himself. And yet, thought, planning and execution guide the sprinter through his or her preparation before a race, determine their tactics out of the blocks, influence their acceleration, their stride, and their energy output. It controls their tempo and their temperament to the finish line. This, surely, is no single-issue machine.

Another example perhaps! One we must surely label a single issue. Let's imagine that you are on a frigate in a war zone, and there is an incoming missile approaching. What do you do? Our instincts say fight or flight.

Taking flight might be possible, but how far would you realistically get? Jumping overboard might get you twenty meters from the ship before the missile strikes. But what of the resulting fireball? What of the flying shrapnel? And if you did survive, what are the odds of rescue? What would be the chances of survival? One in a hundred? One in a thousand? Hardly great odds.

So then to the other side of the coin. If not flight, then to fight. But even in this split-second act of decision-making there are again the questions. With what weapons will we fight? With what tactics? With what projected outcome?

Even in the face of the quickest reactions, tapping our most basic instincts there is thought. How we expand our thought process from the grips of the single-issue machine may be determined by circumstance and events, but coming to terms with it we must.

Approaches to Thought

There are dozens of different thought processes, or, as I call them, approaches to thinking.

From abstract to analytical, from intuitive to cognitive, from emotional to critical, thought has been studied empirically, theoretically and hypothetically.

Dr. Edward de Bono had his 'Six Thinking Hats'. Paul Sloane brought us lateral thinking. Carl Jung talked about intuitive thinking.

Scientists have broken it down from the creative and the subliminal to the persuasive, the realistic, the pragmatic and the idealistic.

An athlete may use visualization before an event to reinforce the outcome. A runner might visualize his or her race from start to finish, from the point of acceleration to the last burst at the finish. A golfer might visualize the flight of his or her ball and its eventual position on the course.

An engineer might use analytical thinking in building a bridge, equating accuracy, thoroughness, and attention to detail while gathering data that he or she rationally and methodically applies to the problem.

A salesman might be a pragmatic thinker, someone who is flexible and resourceful and who looks for immediate payoff rather than for a grand plan that will somehow change the world.

Your approach to thought is uniquely your own. It may be a combination of several approaches. But it begins with a conscious process of identifying a style of thinking, then acknowledging both the strengths and weaknesses of the approach, and finally learning to use it consistently.

Key to the study of thought and the various approaches to thinking is an awareness of how the decision-making process is affected. Once you grasp and understand more clearly the approach of thought that is best suited to you, your decision-making will become more consistent and your contributions to the world will be more defined.

Divisive Thinking

While the term divisive can literally be taken to mean disruptive or combative, it means something much more positive and useful with regard to thought or thinking.

We humans are creatures of habit. We unconsciously map out a path through our lives, acting upon things that we no longer truly think about. In my case, for example, I wake up in the morning, start the coffee, stumble into the bathroom, shave, shower and brush my teeth. This is habitual behavior that requires little thinking. It is a routine, something I do automatically and repetitively, and, therefore, with relative success.

Some things, such as walking or balancing, are so habitual that they have been embedded into our brains as reflexes. Walking is a skill that each of us learns: it is not pre-programmed or automatic. Yet the transition from my bed, down the hall and into the kitchen does not require me to do anything other than look out for walls or misplaced furniture in an attempt to save me from bruises.

A thought becomes an idea, an idea becomes an action, and an action repeated becomes a habit. A habit internalized becomes a reflex. At that point, we have freed ourselves from unnecessary thinking, but is that a good thing or a bad thing?

In some cases, repetition is a good thing. Repetition is a means of improving certain skills and becoming more proficient in our jobs, more skilled in our artistic pursuits, and more in tune to our pursuit of happiness.

But routine and repetition can also hinder our thought process. And that is the very point behind divisive thinking. We need something to help us break out of these habitual processes if we are to become more effective in our thinking, more creative, more inspired. We need something that disrupts or combats routine and automatic behavior.

I call this a thinking device. Compare it, if you will, to the various electrical or mechanical devices that dominate our lives every day, those devices that help us with tasks from the mundane to the amazing. A wristwatch, for example, allows us to keep meetings, catch trains, and stay on task. A key opens the locks to our homes and keeps us secure. A cellular phone allows us to converse with someone across town or on the other side of the world.

A thinking device is much the same. It could be a talisman that we wear around our necks or a smooth stone that we keep in our pockets. It could be an hourly reminder from our cell phones or a musical alarm on our computers. It could be anything that reminds us to go beyond our daily routine, to think outside the box, and to push the envelope of our thought.

Ironically, this thinking device then becomes a habit in its own right. It becomes a technique that is embedded in our daily lives that disrupts and combats routine. If used properly, it reminds us to break away from the mundane. If used properly, it restores the vitality of thought and invigorates our view of the world around us.

It is often said that if you think you are strong, then strong you will become. If you think you are weak, then that is what you will become. One who thinks foolishly, becomes a fool. If you focus on the courageous, you can become more courageous. If you decide to build bridges or design cars, your thoughts can take you there.

Wherever you choose to go, thinking makes everything achievable, but only if we take it beyond the routine and the mundane.

The Law of Thirds

The human brain is predisposed to thinking in terms of threes. The brain absorbs information most effectively in thirds. Our memories are most effective in remembering information that is broken down in lists of three.

If things seem to occur to you on a regular basis in groups of threes, it's because your brain in its most natural state is thinking that way. Speaking of thirds, here are some insights that will lead us further into the book:

- Rather than trying to change the natural processes of your brain, recognize that by adapting your thinking into thirds you will be working in harmony with your brain. The results are extraordinary
- Part of life is communicating with our fellow man. The good news is that their brains operate, by and large, the same way ours do. If you employ the Law of Thirds in your communications, you will naturally be able to engage others more effectively, even if they themselves are not familiar with the Law of Thirds
- The Law of Thirds is a natural problem-solving mechanism, as you will see the further into these pages we travel, so you should never be reluctant to employ it as such.

Let us look at these points in more detail.

We've touched on the way the brain operates already; its desire to internalize processes into habits and reactions. We are inherently lazy. Thinking is expensive. It takes effort, causes stress and consumes our time. The thinking process can actually be summed up in one word – correlation – this is what the brain is actually seeking so much of the time. When I do something, something else happens. When I flick the light switch, the lamp illuminates.

Our brains love simple correlations like the light and light switch; they involve a minimum amount of effort and produce an exceptionally empowering result. If life only involved the switching of light switches, we'd have a very easy lifestyle. Or, alternatively, we would be unstoppable in our capabilities.

In the brain's search for correlation, the brain regurgitates memories, looking for events from our past that can help facilitate understanding. It dissects the problem, breaking it down into the how, why, who, what, and last but not least, the when. When a correlation is found, it is saved. This correlation then becomes a skill; it creates growth to our personalities. It endears confidence; it provides relief.

The brain loves to collect and to categorize, to fill in missing gaps. It has a propensity to subdivide, to simplify and to rationalize. Journeys are re-lived, recalling each and every turn in the road. Every way point is visualized. The result is that our wonderful brains not only expect to retrieve and utilize this knowledge at a later date, it hopes to do so.

The dissection process always ends in a result, or, rather, it ends in three inevitable results: a collection of new information;

a vehicle for changing our perception; and means of adding to our experience.

An important fact to remember in analyzing the Law of Thirds is that the number three cannot be divided. Mathematically speaking it's the first odd prime number, which makes it pretty tricky to subdivide further. Division into thirds of any idea, problem or task you may have is the way your brain is designed to operate. Just as in the way you learnt to walk, and use your legs in the way nature intended them to function, the Law of Thirds will show you how to think and use your brain naturally.

So that's me sorted, I'm thinking just as nature intended, I can go and run a mental marathon now, rather than be stuck crawling around like an infant in a ditch. But all my co-workers are down at that level, I need to communicate with them. They need ideas from me, will they understand this new language?

The answer is of course yes. While you and I don't have Usain Bolt's physique or the power of his legs, we are all fundamentally similar: joints in the same place, same muscle groups, same nervous system sending messages to the legs. We may even have the same desire to do great things.

And so the brains of your colleagues and associates at work are built the same as yours. The foundations for using the Law of Thirds are there; all you have to do is tap into them. And the best way to do this is by employing the concepts we'll be discussing throughout this book. The good news is that when we communicate in thirds, we bypass the listener's conscious dissection of our message. What we say will sound empathic to them, even if they are unaware of how it is happening. Our message, by the very nature of our presentation, will be absorbed more easily. Our listeners will see our points of view as pertinent and well-conceived, and they will remember what we say. What could be better!

Here is the point in a nutshell. We are most effective in our communications with others when applying the Law of Thirds – even if they are unaware of the concept – simply because their brains are also programmed around the Law of Thirds.

All great orators know there are no hidden qualifications required to be a good listener. In fact, nothing is lost on someone with a basic education; a simple understanding of the language is all that is required.

Of course, communication is not reserved for words alone. If your field is not written or spoken, using thirds will make sense, whether it is in a design or business strategy.

The Law of Thirds of course is nothing new. In much of the classical world, buildings can be found with three windows on each wall, or an odd number at least. Similarly the 'golden ratio' is based on a similar concept to the Law of Thirds – yet in two dimensions. A mechanism to stop the brain dividing a rectangle into squares; fold a piece of A4 paper in half and it holds the same ratio of width to height – the brain halts its natural desire to divide. The brain can focus on the words written on the paper.

You will see examples of this natural thought process throughout this book. Some will be highly relevant to you. Others will pique your imagination. All will help you formulate the thinking device needed to become a successful practitioner of the Law of Thirds.

So rather than trying to change your brain – an impossibility to be sure – I will instead encourage you to adapt and train your thinking according to the Law of Thirds, and, in doing so, you will find a synergy that is natural and in accordance with how your brain works in its more natural state.

Two, Four to Twenty-four

Rather than delve straight into the study and application of the Law of Thirds, let's look at other natural divisions and how they naturally succumb to the power of threes.

We noted the division fail of single-issue thinking. We talked about how stifling this is, how easy it is to get stuck in a rut, how machine-like we can become when we focus on a single issue.

But single-issue thinking is not the only source of division fail.

The mind does not see numbers such as two and four as orderly or complete. There is either too much or too little in terms of information. The mind gets bored on the one hand, or overly taxed on the other. The mind does its best work when we allow it to process naturally, and the most natural approach is in factors of three.

Thinking in terms of two is unsatisfying for several reasons. The mind, for one, is not sufficiently stimulated by sets of two. Bored, the mind wanders easily. Moreover, two is generally not sufficient in terms of information required for creative thinking or problem solving. Two is an inanimate set; a pair of wineglasses kept in their box, too expensive to use or throw away, not enough to give to guests. Or that ink pen and pencil set you won at school, the pen of questionable quality needing ink you didn't have, and a retracting pencil far more difficult to use than your 2HB.

When dealing with sets of four, the mind does not take equal issue with all four parts or elements. One is almost assuredly forgotten. The forgotten one becomes, invariably, the unheard one, the one without influence who, in the end, always goes along with what the other three decide.

Four is the beginning of information overload for most approaches to thought. The thought process is more likely to give more weight to one part or one element to the detriment of another.

You can extrapolate from these division failures how additional issues or elements of five or more affect the thought process. Imagine how the mind reacts when bombarded by lists or subdivisions of six or eight or ten.

For our purposes, the important point to remember is that the brain is always adding or subtracting from lists of two, four, or more – whichever the case may be – to satisfy the Law of Thirds.

The following illustrations are but a preview of endless lists, subsets, or subdivisions of twos, fours, and more, and I encourage you to create your own examples.

Remember, this exploration into the Law of Thirds is not about a single function or discipline. There is no end to the possibilities, from art to science, from outdoor sports to indoor activities, from medicine to law, from music to musings, from politics to poetry, I will touch on only as many as is needed to demonstrate our findings, but encourage you to see the breadth of the study. It is essentially without end.

Your exploration will provide further evidence of The Law of Thirds' inevitable influence, but let's begin with these.

Two

The study of two seems too obvious in many respects. That is until you look a little deeper.

The Taoist concept of Yin and Yang is an excellent example. Yin and Yang symbolize the balance that exists in all nature. Beauty and ugliness define one another. Tall and short can only be described in relationship to each other. Strong and weak, hot and cold, happy and sad. And yet for everything that we characterize as black and white, there is a nothingness, or an interaction, or a gray area that remains true to our most natural thought process. Think about how this works in your daily life. There are rarely only two sides to an issue, two explanations for why things occur, two solutions for any mystery. For every pro and every con, there is a third, less defined option.

We talk about right and wrong as if nothing in between exists, and yet right and wrong are simply two opinions characterized by a third element: the middle ground. We can never truly know right and wrong because there are always mitigating circumstances that shade the truth or help explain the indiscretion.

There is never just a beginning and an end, despite our emphasis on the two. "When did this all begin?" "How will it end?" Once we allow our natural thought process to engage, we see clearly that there is a beginning, a middle, and an end.

We have a past and a future, but we live in the present. You can't have one without the other two; the Law of Thirds won't allow it.

In a court of law, there is the plaintiff and the defense who may define the conflict, but it is the judge, that most important third element, that creates the potential for justice. Even in arbitration, it is the third party, the arbitrator or the mediator, who makes the interaction possible.

A conversation can be defined as two people in discussion. One is talking while the other is listening. But from the perspective of an individual and the Law of Thirds, both parties are actually talking, or listening, or waiting to talk, eager to get his or her point across. We know that the ability to keep quiet and to focus on what is being said is not only an important skill, but it actually enhances your ability to respond once it is your turn to chime in. Yet we cannot eliminate from a conversation this position we call waiting to talk, or there would be no conversation.

Let's look into the western psyche to explore what has become atypical of our world view. We are a society that places extraordinary emphasis on winning and losing. And yet a more complete picture is drawn of this highly emphasized mindset when we add the all-important third component: win, lose, or draw.

As it turns out, we've got used to the idea that not every situation produces a winner and loser. In the game of soccer, you actually get a point for a tie game. The same holds true for hockey. We are now obsessed with what we call the tie-breaker, and even a tie-breaker sometimes fails to produce a winner.

Are dead heats in such things as horse racing and Olympic sprints not the most exciting of events? Would a ten-round heavyweight-boxing match that ended in a draw not be rated an unparalleled occurrence? Draws, in whatever the competition might be – from sporting events to school debates – deserve equal recognition and appreciation to those accorded great wins and drubbing defeats.

Even wars rarely end up with a clear-cut winner. There is almost always a negotiated settlement that really defines how a conflict ends. Maybe that's why people are so easily seduced by armed conflict.

In business, the terms profit and loss are the cornerstones defining success and failure. And yet, it's not always about turning a profit; sometimes you're satisfied just to break even, the ability to maintain an account balance that allows the business to continue functioning, to stay afloat, to fight another year. Most of us would admit that treading water doesn't sound so bad, especially in economic hard times and especially considering the alternative.

Here is one we don't often consider. We often hear the saying is the glass half empty, or is it half full? This is supposed to define whether you are a particularly positive person or a negative one. Logically, however, the saying is misleading and should be rewritten as, is the glass half empty, half full, or twice as large as it needs to be? Now the mind has something to work with.

We define a couple, traditionally, as a man and a woman. But we define the family unit, traditionally, as a man, woman, and child. There is something congruous and stable about such a revered trinity.

Two is a wonderful number that is almost always subject to the Law of Thirds. More importantly, it is a number that only touches the surface of our brain's most potent approach to thought.

Challenge yourself. Satisfy your brain's thirst for fuller, more fulfilling explorations by pushing past the constraints of the number two. Most importantly, get into sync with the natural processes of the Law of Thirds and really start thinking.

Four

From two to four! It seems like a small step, but it's not so small when it comes to the natural processes of the brain, not to mention the magical prowess of the Law of Thirds lurking in between.

There are four sides to a square and four wheels on a car (well, most cars), but for most of us who live in the West, the first thing that comes to mind when someone poses a question about the number four is the four seasons; the undisputed division of the year, each transition marked by a scientific event, an interaction of the sun and the earth, the dependable geometry of the planets.

Well, at least that's one way to look at it. The question is: for whom does this so-called fact serve? As a topical science lesson for inattentive middle-schoolers? As the title for a timeless piece of music made famous by a Venetian composer? Or perhaps as the ever-recognizable name for a world-class hotel franchise?

Historically, the four seasons were of great importance, of course. The measuring of the solstice and equinox were fundamental components for many religions and corresponding civilizations, thus we confer that the measurement and conveyance of these dates was the preserve of the political elite, which is surely enough to make most of us suspicious, if not downright incredulous.

It also begs the question; are these four seasons of any use to the general population in this day and age? Can they be used to predict the weather, for instance? Can they be used to accurately determine when events of annual significance should occur? Do they aid in the illumination or the inspiration of the businessman, the artist, the musician, or the educator?

Let's think this through. On the one hand, we have science. On the other, we have social function. And this is where the disjunction is most apparent, and where we begin to see that the seasons of Galileo and Copernicus provide the general populous with little or no benefit. What do we think of with the coming of spring? We picture tulips and daffodils sprouting. Come summer, we fancy picnics under the shade of a tall tree, volleyball in the park, and endless days of wearing shorts and tank tops. Autumn/Fall has always signified changing leaves and the last wisp of life from flowers we planted with such optimism the previous spring. And winter brings to mind endless days of cold and hibernation.

But this is all reverse association. In truth, spring is well underway when the equinox occurs in late March. The solstice does not mark either the longest or the hottest day of the year, at least not in most places in the world. As depressing as it may sound, fall and its magical colors is little more than a blink of the eye, a fortnight around the Columbus Day weekend. If you're planning a trip to view the changing Aspen or the fiery reds of the oak, you'd better do it judiciously or the moment will soon be past.

So while fall is far too quick and never the three months so often attributed to it, winter can drag on and on for months on end.

In Africa, the pattern is one way; in Europe it is another. And yet, the concept of four seasons fits in neither.

So what if we start again, without the scientists and mathematicians dictating what is what and when is when. What if we let our brains decide the seasons?

You will see that our natural thought process instinctively splits the year into thirds. You will see that our brains have already categorized the seasons long before we consciously begin to ponder the issue.

What we call winter can begin as early as October in many parts of the world and could very well be called the 'Dormant Season'. The weather is cold and the nights are long, often restricting outside play, exercise and relaxation. The plants are in hibernation, as are the trees. Winter is often a source of cabin fever. Bears, at least, have figured out that hibernation is the best way to get through a tough winter, while you and I resort to backgammon, television, and the works of Dickens, Tolstoy and Shakespeare.

Just about the time we think we are about to go stir crazy, the season rebirth arrives. Spring and summer are what the scientists call it. This is the time when flowers start to sprout, seeds are sown, and robins, geese and swallows return to build their nests and raise their young. Easter and the perennial flowering of trees launch us into April. May is the month of optimism. June is the month of marriage and the promise of crops to harvest and vegetables to pick. July and August we watch and wait and water, basking in the glory of sunny days and short nights. September hints of cooler weather and the changing light of the sun.

Autumn, a modern word only recently introduced to the lexicon of the seasons by the British, was called "Haervest" back in the 16th century when most people lived off the land. The English who first came to North America brought with them the term 'Fall', a reference to the "falling of the leaves," or "the fall of the season."

Actually, this third and most prominent season – we should call it the Harvest Season – includes the collecting of hay, the picking and canning of fruit and the various and sundry preparations for the winter ahead. It is important to note that the first hay is cut in early June (the medieval month of 'Heymonath'), and harvesting of everything from corn to rhubarb continues through the harvest moon in September right up to the first of October. That's some season.

Okay, so that describes quite nicely the seasons typical of North America and Europe. So how does the rest of the world fit into a three-season – Growing, Harvesting, Dormant – model? Very nicely, in fact.

While much of Asia is tropical, and many an American or European might describe it as hot the whole year round, rest assured that the local population splits the year into thirds, and the thought process is completely natural.

Thailand, for example, spells out the seasons as hot, rainy and cold. In India, there is the tropical climate, the mountain climate and the dry climate. Others have the wet season, the dry season and the hot season. Remember that these delineations have nothing to do with nature conforming to a law; this is the logic of the people; this is an entire population thinking the same way, thinking in accordance with the Law of Thirds.

The truth is, when you look around the globe, from country to country, the seasons are actually marked by three things: weather, ecology and hours of daylight. This isn't science; this is people reacting logically to three forces of nature. Not surprising.

In some parts of the world, special seasons are loosely defined based upon important events such as: hurricane season, tornado season and wildfire season, again tapping man's penchant for thirds.

Astronomers love to talk about the solstices and equinoxes in trying to calculate the seasons. They call them the March Equinox, June Solstice, September Equinox and December Solstice. Some try to convince us that they bisect the seasons; others say the four dates represent the start of the seasons. But the truth is these ponderings are more theoretical than practical and no self-respecting farmer would ever use them for the management of their crops.

More proof needed? Think about the school terms, or the holidays to be more pertinent. Why are school children required to be at home in the middle of winter, several weeks in spring and for almost two months in late summer? Of course the answer is to help out on the family farm; fixing hedges and ditches in winter, planting seeds during Easter and harvesting come late summer. Long after 95% of the population stopped working in agriculture, the natural seasons have left their mark.

So much for the seasons. Let's talk about some other prominent fours that are equally affected by the Law of Thirds. How about these:

There were four Musketeers: Athos, Aramis, Porthos, and d'Artagnan.

The novel of Alex Dumas titled 'The Three Musketeers' was in fact the story of how D'Artagnan became a musketeer. Ask anyone if D'Artagnan was one of the three musketeers and you already know how they're likely to reply.

We've touched on Taoism already and the realm of religion and spirituality will appear several more times whilst upon this numerical journey. The Christian bible is full of many fictitious, almost mythical stories. The Apocalypse of John features many ciphers, including 24 elders, four beasts with six wings apiece, and a very cool lamb with seven horns and seven eyes.

The lamb, as the story is told, goes on to break the seven seals in the Book of Revelation, releasing four horsemen, a devastating earthquake, war without end, famine and plague. Exciting stuff, but it's the Four Horsemen of the Apocalypse who have found infamy on the ceiling of the Sistine chapel, in countless works of fiction and on the silver screen in movies often best forgotten.

Infamy aside, what are the four horseman, what do they represent, and how do we remember them?

To begin with, their horses are white, red, black and pale, symbolizing plague, war, famine and death respectively.

Interestingly, if asked, most people will only be able to recite three of the four apocalyptic events, and few ever remember the pale horse.

After plague, war and famine, plain old death seems a fairly humdrum way to bow out. And what comes later is forgotten universally.

Following such death and destruction, let's look to Buddhism. Hail the four noble truths:

- Life means suffering: sorrow, pain, grief
- The origin of suffering is attachment: to pleasure, lust, longevity
- The cessation of suffering is attainable: be centered, be content, be at peace
- The path to cessation of suffering: wisdom, ethics, concentration.

It might be easier to remember the three schools of Buddhists: Theravada, Vajrayana, and Mahayana. Or the three jewels that Buddhists look for guidance from: Buddha, Sangha, and Dharma. Or the three delusions of mankind: ignorance, despair, and anger.

The point is that our minds think and grasp in sets of three. Your mind naturally breaks things down into thirds, so embracing this in turn creates an invaluable tool for all time.

Five

From science and religion, we move swiftly on to business and economics and the numerical proclivities of the number five.

You've heard of Porter's Five Forces. Or maybe you haven't. Michael Porter is a Harvard professor who identified five competitive forces that shape every single industry and market. These forces look at everything from the intensity of competition to the profitability and attractiveness of an industry. The five are:

- Bargaining power of suppliers
- Bargaining power of customers
- Threat of new entrants
- Threat of substitute products
- Competitive rivalry.

The Law of Thirds makes it much simpler, reducing the five forces to three, and calling them: inputs, outputs and competition. The information, in the end, is the same, but by applying the Law of Thirds it becomes so much more accessible. Moreover, there is now much less to memorize for your Economics 101 exam and that's always a good thing.

We have five senses – seeing, hearing, touching, tasting, and smelling – and they are all wonderful. Our brains, however, generally rely on only three of these at any time. With food, we see, we taste, we smell. With art, we see, we touch, we listen.

In conversation, we hear, see and touch (yes, touch can be one of the strongest forms of signaling agreement, enthusiasm, confidentiality and attraction within a conversation). Our natural thought process finds power, security and inspiration – again a list of three – in melding three senses into the most effective sensory vehicle possible.

Five is a number highly respected in Asian cultures. The Japanese, for example, always use serving sets of five, but, interestingly, three is the preferred number for tea. The Chinese consider a gathering of five a preferred number for social events, but three creates the most effective environment for business discussions. Who knew?

Food comes in five basic tastes. Can you name them? They are sweet, sour, salty, bitter, and umami. Yes, umami, which is another way of saying savory or savoriness. Ask 100 people and most will get stuck after three: sweet, sour, and salty. Bitter and savory are the two most forgotten of the five basic tastes.

Have some fun with this one. Some people claim there are only four basic elements of nature. Others claim there are five. Most people can only name three. Aristotle claimed there were only four basic elements, calling them: water, air, fire and earth. The Chinese would argue that there are five, and they named them: water, wood, metal, fire and earth. When asked, the majority of people will stop at three and most commonly say: earth, wind and fire.

Here's a good one. The five-star constellation Cassiopeia resides in the far northern sky. It circles the polestar Polaris throughout the year and also straddles the Milky Way. The five major stars of Cassiopeia (also known as The Lady of the Chair) are shaped like a "W" (or an "M," depending on your orientation). Unfortunately, only three of its stars can be seen by the naked eye, and then only on the clearest of nights.

Speaking of stars, they are most often drawn with five points, of course, though a really aggressive artist might portray them with six, seven, or even eight points. Yet pay a visit to the Valley of the Kings on the west bank of the Nile and you will find the ceilings of the burial chambers decorated with thousands of three-pointed stars. For my money, I'd say the Egyptians were smarter than the practitioners of witchcraft and Satanism and their affection for sketching pentagrams, but who's to say.

A pentagon has five sides, amphibians, reptiles and the vast majority of humans have five toes or fingers, and one of the most hummable songs ever written is titled Take Five. The Olympic symbol has five interwoven circles, most cars with manual transmissions have five gears.

There are many examples of five and there are any number of examples of our brains reducing these to lists of three. Our amazing brains have a way of sorting through the jumble that so often accompanies lists or subdivisions of five, knowing that the information will be more pertinent in the long run if the list is pared to three.

It is a matter of information overload on the one hand, but also an excess of information on the other. The mind takes what it needs and moves on. Very efficient.

Six

Portmanteau is the name we give to a word made of two or more other words. Permaculture is such a word, constructed from permanent and agriculture by a gentleman named Josef (Sepp) Holzer in the 1960s. But before we discuss the meaning of this unusual word, let's talk a little about Sepp and his farm.

Sepp has a 45-hectare farm in Austria, 1800 meters above sea level, so we'd describe him as a mountain farmer. At this altitude, farming is traditionally quite minimal; grazing cattle is normally the only activity that is attempted. A self-styled 'Rebel Farmer,' Sepp experimented with modifications to the landscape to allow more productive farming in this restrictive environment.

He coined the term 'six permaculture zones'. The six zones are used when trying to find a balance between the places where humans live and where plants and animals should be raised to achieve balance. They are generally listed as:

1. The place we live – for decorative plants and domesticated animals only
2. Places that must be visited often – for cultivated vegetables primarily and animals such as chickens
3. Places that must be visited occasionally – for fruit bearing plants and grazing animals

4. Places that need a large area — for groves and herd animals like cows
5. Semi wild area — for wild plants and herd animals like horses
6. Wild area — for everything else.

But in reading this list, our brain once again seeks, not so much to rationalize, but to categorize and organize, to prioritize what is most useful, while giving credence to the whole.

Because zone zero represents the place where we live, our most natural thought process will exclude it from a list focusing on 'permanent agriculture'. Similarly, our brains will naturally eliminate zones 5 and 6 from the equation since both have considerably less farming benefit than zones 2, 3 and 4. And thus, we are now aligned with the Law of Thirds and equipped with information of true relevance.

In fact, the mind might very well look at Sepp's list, dissect it, and build two groups of thirds that work separately as well as side by side. For instance:

- Urban area — place for living
- Farm area — for crops and livestock
- Wild area — left to nature.

Then the brain processes the contents of zones 5 and 6 and neatly and seamlessly applies the Law of Thirds and inserts a new classification. The result is:

- Semi wild area — husbanded and informal harvesting
- Wild area — left to nature
- Extremely wild area — inaccessible jungle.

What we have done is create a hierarchical relationship between the zones. While we might very well be able to commit the six zones of Sepp's original list to memory using rote memorization, applying thirds to the equation allows the brain to remember the various collections automatically, with simple triggers like urban, farm, or wild.

More importantly, the information is now more accessible as a tool, as useful on the farm as it would be in the classroom. And having a little fun with it, guess what happens when you send a hundred people out to the fields with a bag of plant seed in their hands? You guessed it: 90% of them will put three seeds in each drill hole.

Looking beyond the worlds of agriculture and urbanism, we see also that geography is also well served by the simplicity and attractiveness of the Law of Thirds.

"How so?" you might ask. Take, for instance, Peveril Meigs' wonderfully tidy classification of the world's deserts into extremely arid, arid, and semi-arid. While there is almost a childish simplicity to this, it is the universally recognized classification system. Why? Because everyone understands when you classify things into three!

The six classifications of forests are often referred to as boreal, temperate, tropical, sub-tropical, old growth and second growth. Be serious. Who remembers those? Not anyone I know. In fact, the vast majority of people very appropriately scrub this gangly list in favor of a more manageable, more useful list of three: evergreen (or coniferous), deciduous (or broadleaf) and mixed. Now that was easy.

When we talk about ecology, we are referring to what the Greeks call living relations, the three interrelated studies that scientists use to study them: distribution, abundance and shared effects.

In American football, a touchdown counts for six points. But far more games are decided by a field goal, which counts for only three points, than by a touchdown.

In music, there are six strings on a guitar (12 strings in some cases and four on a ukulele). However, the most common chords on all three such instruments are created using three fingers.

In religion, there are six articles of belief in the Islamic faith, but there are only three holy cities in which practicing Muslims make their pilgrimages: Mecca, Medina, and Jerusalem.

Yes, there are six packs (beer and abs), but they hardly belong together. Drinking more than three beers in a sitting will get you looking like what the Indonesians call 'tiga gunung' (three mountains). There are six degrees of separation. There are six dynasties. Six is the highest number on a dice and the highest number in Dominoes. There are six men on an ice hockey team.

But the truth is, six turns out to be an unwieldy number when it comes to information and our brains tend to weed out the important parts from those parts it feels are less relevant, very often employing the Law of Thirds.

Seven

The number seven has a certain allure about it. Maybe it comes from the craps tables in Las Vegas or Monte Carlo where rolling a seven can be the number of success as well as the number of doom. Maybe it's the fact that there are seven days in a week.

Or maybe it's because there are seven colors in the rainbow. Can you name them? Red, orange, yellow, green, blue, indigo and violet. Those, of course, are also the seven colors produced by a three-sided prism. An equally interesting fact is that color televisions have been engineered to display all seven colors of the rainbow as well, and they do so by shooting three electron beams out of the cathode ray tube to the flat screen. Here's the interesting part: each of these three beams has a name: red beam, green beam and blue beam. We will revisit this fact a bit later in the book, but for now, onto the greatest writer of all time and one of his contributions to the Law of Thirds.

Shakespeare, as we know, wrote about the seven ages of man – apparently he never got around to expounding upon the various ages of women. In this enigmatic poem, he takes us on a journey through our lives, beginning with the mewling and puking of infancy, through the whining and shining of boyhood, and onto the sighing and woeful lover. The journey takes us jealous and quarrelsome soldier, to the round and wise justice of adulthood, and onto what he labels the bespectacled and paunchy pantaloon. Coming full circle, we end our lives in a second childhood, oblivious and toothless.

But Shakespeare must have known that a list of such expanded references would be challenged by the Law of Thirds, because he then went on to proclaim, "All the world's a stage. And all the men and women merely players." This fits perfectly into the natural ability of our brains to take the seven ages of men, blend them with the idea of men and women on the world's stage and create a myriad of temporal divisions ever-present in our lives. Here are a few of the more obvious:

- Single – Married – Widowed
- Student – Worker – Retiree
- Born Alone – Live Alone – Die Alone.

Shakespeare was a poet. His wonderful poem about the seven ages of man paints such an evocative picture that we can instantly envision man as he evolves from infancy to adulthood and back again, childish once more. But the Law of Thirds absolutely plays an important role as we read the poem. The mind subconsciously splits the passing images described by the poet into thirds. As Shakespeare adds a new stage, the mind registers only the most recent three, dropping them age to age, until we are left with the last three and an overwhelming sense of our lives passing us by.

So much for poetry. What about politics? The U.S. Constitution is built around seven articles, those describing the Legislative Branch, the Executive Branch, the Judicial Branch, the States, Amendments, Debts (Supremacy and Oaths) and Ratification. Ask a sampling of Americans to name the seven, and you will quickly find that almost all are stumped once you get beyond — you guessed it — the three branches of government.

The seventh amendment to the Constitution touts an American's right to a trial by jury but it is a phrase consisting of three simple concepts that is considered by many as part of one of the most well-crafted, influential sentences in the history of the English language, exalting three unalienable rights worth fighting for: life, liberty, and the pursuit of happiness.

Everyone knows the seven deadly sins, right? Wrath, greed, sloth, pride, lust, envy and gluttony. Created long ago just to remind the masses of their wayward tendencies, parents and teachers from ages past would spend hours drumming the seven into the heads of school kids whose brains were quickly rejecting them. Most of us continue to reject them as well. Ask the same sampling of Americans that we quizzed about the articles above to name the seven deadly sins, and few will recite more than three. Those most often listed? Greed, lust and envy of course.

It also makes sense, if you use your imagination, that if there are seven deadly sins then there should be seven un-deadly virtues. Are they as hard to name as the seven sins? Try your hand, and then take a look at this auspicious list: chastity, temperance, charity, diligence, kindness, patience and humility. I managed charity, patience and humility, and I am assuming that my natural thought process sees these as the most important three for my life.

That's how the Law of Thirds works. The mind is our friend. It doesn't confuse us with too much information nor bore us with too little.

We mentioned in an earlier section the affinity of various Asian cultures with odd numbers. Seven is the number most often related to the seeking of truth. The Japanese created their seven lucky gods or the seven gods of good fortune. The god of abundance, the god of longevity, the god of wealth, the god of warriors, the god of the arts, the god of happiness and the god of fishers. Modern Japan has reduced this list to three: the god of health, wealth and longevity; the god of abundance, good health and pleasure; and the god of knowledge, art and beauty. Notice how the three are also lists of three. Very clever and very convenient. In America, all telephone numbers are seven digits with a three digit area code. However, to call someone somewhere else in the world, you'll need a country code, an area code, and a local number. And by the same logic, I could call someone locally using only the local code, or the area code plus local code, or indeed using the full international number. Confusing, but convenient.

To call the American Embassy in Paris, for example, you'd be dialing 01-43-12-22-22 (note how the French split the number into pairs), whereas the embassy in Tokyo would be 03-3224-5000, London is 020-7499-9000 and Shanghai is 21-6433-3936. What's the relationship here to the Law of Thirds? Most people naturally split numbers as long and cumbersome as a telephone number into three parts, or better still groups of three numbers. This is no accident.

Want to call the emergency services? Or connect with an operator? Around the world, the emergency codes most preferred when calling an ambulance or reporting a life or death situation tap directly into the Law of Thirds. For example, you dial 911 in the US, 999 in the UK, 144 in Switzerland, 112 in Europe and 000 in Australia. Pretty obvious.

Sure, there are exceptions. Take Oman, the country in the Middle East that piggybacks Saudi Arabia and isn't high on most people's list of most desirable places to visit: emergency code (9999). And then there's South Africa, home of gold and diamond mines and a place many of us would enjoy visiting: emergency code 10177. Okay, and yes, French Guyana and Morocco both use 15.

But what about the global emergency number used by the GSM system? Emergency code 112, a welcome return to the Law of Thirds.

There are seven digits in a million dollars; well, there are if you ignore the cents, and since there are no cents in a million dollars, it's easy to ignore. But how do we write a million dollars? $1,000,000. That's right. Whenever we write an amount larger than $999, we add a delimiter called a thousands separator. No, the separator itself is not universal – Americans use a comma, Germans use dots, Arabic uses a hamza that looks like a quotation mark, and Australians use a half space – but the splitting of the groups into three digits is very much universal. Why? Because the brain works the same in every country, every culture, and every ethnic group.

And what would a list of seven be without the seven wonders of the world. That is a quiz that few of us can pass. Ask a friend, ask your boss, ask your secretary. You'll probably get three different answers, but you can rest assured that whoever you ask, few will be able to name more than three. Try it yourself, then peruse the full list below:

- Stonehenge
- The Coliseum in Rome
- The Great Wall of China
- Catacombs of Kom el Shoqafa
- The Taj Mahal
- The Great Pyramid of Giza
- Hagia Sophia.

How did you do? Most commonly mentioned are the Great Wall, the Great Pyramid and Stonehenge. Or did you say, the Hanging Gardens of Babylon or the Lighthouse of Alexandria? You may well have, because no one really knows what the seven wonders categorically are. Time has erased all but a few references to the original list, a sort of Chinese whispering across the centuries. But arguing over the list is half the fun. It still doesn't change the fact that few of us ever get past the list of three that our brains have hung onto since we were first introduced to the seven wonders back in junior school.

Seven, under any circumstances, is a special number. It's also an unwieldy number. Seven of anything is a lot of information. Our brains rarely describe things in groups of seven. We rarely express our views in lists of seven. But what we often do is pare a list of seven down for purposes of study and communication, and most often those pared down lists are directly influenced by the Law of Thirds.

Eight

The number eight gets far less attention than seven, but not because it is necessarily less significant.

The Beatles made us believe that a real commitment to love was something that wasn't just a 24/7 thing, but rather an eight days a week thing.

And while the number eight is considered good fortune in many cultures, Buddhists have made it a way of life with the eightfold path. What are the eight?

- Know the truth (wisdom)
- Control your thoughts (wisdom)
- Say nothing to hurt others (ethics)
- Respect life (ethics)
- Work for good of others (ethics)
- Practice meditation (concentration)
- Resist evil (concentration)
- Free the mind of evil (concentration).

As meaningful and insightful as these paths are, modern-day Buddhists have since divided the eight to fit the natural thought process of the Law of Thirds. The result is three paths commonly referred to as wisdom, ethical conduct and concentration. This does not diminish the power of the eight; in fact, it allows the mind to approach them with greater emphasis. For example, concentration is now the source of its own list of three: practice meditation, resist evil and free the mind of evil.

We've all heard, "Blessed are the meek." We can quote, "Blessed are the poor in spirit." And we remember, "Blessed are the peacemakers." What we often forget is that these three well-recognized phrases are part of a more impressive list called the eight Beatitudes, made famous by a speech given by Jesus Christ called the Sermon on the Mount and also paraphrased in the Dead Sea Scrolls. Pretty lofty stuff.

The Eight Ball is the most famous and most important ball on a pool table; pocketing the eight ball before sinking (or "potting," as the English say) all the solids (spots in the UK) or stripes (as in the game we call Eight Ball) is the quickest way to end a game and doesn't make you look very good in front of your friends or the girl you're trying to impress. But like everything else, cue sports, as we call games played with a cue stick and billiard balls, is broken up into three major subdivisions. Can you name them? They are:

- Carom billiards, referring to games played on tables without pockets
- Pool, generally played on a table with six pockets
- Snooker, also a pocket game, but with a completely different array of balls than traditional pool.

But when someone says you're behind the eight ball, it doesn't have anything to do with pool; it means you're in a bad situation, that you're out of luck, or that you're up the creek without a paddle. If someone refers to you as an Eightball as in, "Man, you're a real eightball," I wouldn't take it as a compliment. They're probably trying to tell you that you've got a loose screw, are in some way playing with less than a full deck, or are just downright peculiar. Like I said, not a compliment.

The term Section 8 has a couple of meanings. The first and most commonly used is as an expression that describes what happens when the military boots you out of the Army or the Navy or some other arm of the service because you've been deemed mentally unfit to carry a gun or drive a tank. "You're a Section 8" is also one of those phrases that should not be looked at as a compliment.

With that in mind, I have to ask: what happened to sections one through to seven? Forgotten and unimportant? Answer: unknown. However, there is still an important list of three generated by the military's rather nebulous discharge mechanism. There is the aforementioned Section 8, which really doesn't look good on a résumé. There is the Dishonorable Discharge, which looks even worse on a résumé. And there is the General Discharge (leaving under "honorable" conditions) and this, at least, isn't likely to put off a potential employer, hinder the serviceman from finding alternative employment, or impair his ability to re-enlist in another service. This is the 'middle ground' or 'gray area' that we talked about in section Two. It serves the purpose in a constructive and enabling way.

In the US, the term Section 8 also refers to an ill-conceived housing assistance program dreamed up by the Federal Government during the Great Depression that was broken into three subdivisions: new construction, substantial rehabilitation and existing housing. Sounds good on the surface, right? But like most government programs, it went awry because nobody understood what anyone else was doing – even though there were only three subdivisions – and probably led to the military adopting Section 8 to describe guys who were unfit to carry guns and drive tanks. Makes sense to me.

You've heard of a figure of eight knot, so named because it looks like an eight when it's tied. But did you know that the knot only requires three basic steps:

- Form a loop in the rope
- Bring the end around the rope
- Pass the end through the loop and pull.

Voila! A figure eight!

You've heard of eight patrons of the zodiac. Or maybe you haven't. These are the guys who look after the 12 astrological animals associated with the Chinese calendar and who are in direct conflict with the three monkeys, known as:

- Speak No Evil
- Hear No Evil
- See No Evil.

Leave it to the Chinese to simplify a list of eight patrons that few can identify and 12 zodiac figures that are really only important if your birthday happens to land in their year – as in Year of the Dog – by using the Law of Thirds. The result is a list of three that even young children have no trouble remembering.

No, eight doesn't always equal three, but you can see how often our brains simplify a cumbersome equation or break down something worthy of our most natural approach to thought.

Hopefully you're not too confused by all of this, because now we turn our attention to even greater heights, or at least an even greater opportunity for confusion. Welcome to the world of nine.

Nine

Nine has more connections to three than any other number. Three squared equals nine. Three plus three plus three equals nine. Nine divided by three equals three. The normal pregnancy cycle for a woman is nine months broken into three trimesters. You get the picture.

There are nine planets. That is how most of us divide and describe our solar system. But where do we place the sun, asteroids, or comets in that case? Division of the nine planets has been attempted in many ways and often using the Law of Thirds. For example, in the age of Ptolemy, earth was still at the center of the universe. Inferior planet and superior planet groupings categorized them with relation to the earth.

Rock, ice, and gas planets – does that sound too naive for planetary physics? How about terrestrial, ice giant and Jovian; the name Jovian, just to keep things tidy, derived from Jupiter.

More modern classification is also by composition; gas giants include Jupiter, Saturn, Uranus and Neptune – that's right, the icy and extraordinarily cold Uranus and Neptune got categorized as gassy! Very scientific!

Then there are the inner planets; Mercury, Venus, Earth and Mars. The word 'inner' describes their position to the asteroid belt. This is of interest in and of itself. The planet

"Cerere Ferdinandea" (Ceres) was discovered at the turn of the 19th century inside the asteroid belt and was classified with great fanfare as the eighth planet. And it remained so for many years.

What about the dwarf planets? They include Pluto the so called tenth planet. Then we have Eris, Sedna, Quaoar, Haumea, Makemake, Orcus and an estimated 400 other undiscovered planets. That's a lot of planets. And don't forget Charon; yes, now we refer to it as the moon of Pluto. All very confusing.

We also list our planets according to their time of discovery, such as:

- Classical planets (Mercury, Venus, Mars, Jupiter and Saturn)
- Modern planets (Uranus and Neptune)
- Day of reckoning planets (Earth and Pluto).

Why Pluto, you ask? Because one day of reckoning some years back it was relegated to a dwarf planet. Why Earth? Because if we don't get it right pretty soon, a day of reckoning is just around the corner.

Strictly speaking, there were nine planets from the year 1930 – when Pluto was discovered – to 2000 when the Hayden Planetarium removed Pluto from its exhibit.

Or, were there ever nine planets anyway? The word planet is Greek for wanderer meaning any celestial object that moves against the backdrop of stars. So by that definition, are we really saying that the earth is not a planet? Hope not!

Bring on the committee!

In 2005 a committee was formed to untangle the mess. And guess what, three definitions were used to define what makes a planet.

Cultural, structural and dynamical. That is, people must think of it as a planet. It must be spherical and it must not be surrounded by a lot of rocky detritus.

Not the most practical approach and one that led to numerous arguments; which is what scientists and committees do best. They disagree. Well, after that, another committee proposed three options for a definitive definition, it was the second of those options that stood. It reads:

"A planet is a celestial body that (a) has sufficient mass for its self-gravity to overcome rigid body forces so that it assumes a hydrostatic equilibrium (nearly round) shape, and (b) is in orbit around a star, and is neither a star nor a satellite of a planet." IAU 2006

And if you believe that without equivocation, we're left with twelve planets, a nice round number.

But how many are there right now? The answer, you'll be surprised, perturbed or just plain disappointed to hear is eight. Using thirds to change the status quo can make you unpopular!

Enough astronomy. Let's talk felines and philosophy.

In Japan, the number nine is avoided as often as possible because it symbolizes suffering, whereas the number three symbolizes balance.

Cats have nine lives. But the reason cats have nine lives is because they possess three exceptional traits:

- Exceptionally keen sense of balance
- Exceptionally keen sense of sight, smell, and hearing
- Exceptional agility.

Nine is not a number to be disrespected. But it is still a number highly susceptible to the incontrovertible Law of Thirds.

Nine appeals to the brain in particular because it can so easily be broken down into three groups of three. But make no mistake, the ease with which nine can be manipulated, broken down, or divided is more mathematical than it is practical, and the Law of Thirds is nothing if not practical. That's why our brains rely on it so heavily in its approach to the task of thought.

Ten

Ten is the number of convenience. Ten is the number we all use when really we're not sure whether a list or a grouping really contains anywhere between eight and twelve items, events, situations, people, or whatever the things happen to be. "Oh, around ten, I guess."

Whenever someone puts together their list of favorite things, like movies, or songs, or football teams, it's always a Top Ten list. The year's Top Ten list of best movies. The Top Ten reasons why men and women don't get along. My Top Ten favorite sporting events of all time. You get the gist. But ironically – though not surprisingly – we never give out awards for the Top Ten of anything. We almost always award the top three in any event. The Olympic Games, of course, epitomizes this with the awarding of gold, silver, and bronze medals. But even in the World Cup soccer tournament, teams are recognized for their first, second and third place finishes.

Speaking of games, there are ten pins in bowling. Ten pins because ten is the perfect number for building the pyramid that forms the target at the end of the lane. But once again, the Law of Thirds is the dominating principle in succeeding at this everyman game, because it is the three pins at the head of the pyramid that our brains tell us to aim at. Hit those and very likely the rest of the pins will fall. Miss those and you have no chance at bowling a strike.

From sports to religion, we explore the Ten Commandments. (The Greeks, by the way, call them the Ten Matters and Hebrew calls them the Ten Words.) No need to list them here and I won't ask you to name them. Why? Because most of us can't name all ten, not if your last catechism class was as long ago as mine was. But what most of us can do is name three of the ten. Ask 100 people and the three you'll most often hear?

- Thou shalt honor your father and mother
- Thou shalt not commit adultery
- Thou shalt not steal.

Interestingly, it doesn't take much research to realize that there are several reliable sources that list as many as 16 commandments, including the books of Exodus and Deuteronomy; pretty credible sources, right?

Among the most interesting excluded from the ten most often cited?

- Exodus 20:23: Ye shall not make with me gods of silver, neither shall ye make unto you gods of gold
- Exodus 20:26: And do not go up to my altar on steps, lest your nakedness be exposed on it
- Exodus 20:4: You shall not make for yourself an idol, whether in the form of anything that is in heaven above, or that is on the earth beneath, or that is in the water under the earth.

Notice anything familiar? Yes, another list of three.

The numbers one to ten form the basis of our counting system. This is universal throughout the world, but when they are arranged on the key pad of a cell phone, a keyboard, or a TV remote, guess what? They are arranged in rows of three, with the zero placed conveniently below. This way, we can change channels without ever taking our eyes off the screen.

You've heard the expression; she's a ten, referring to a pretty girl. Or, that was a ten, in reference to the perfect meal or a great vacation. Ten is that number that we use when rating something or someone at the highest level.

Three, on the other hand, is considered far luckier than ten. The Chinese consider three a lucky number because it sounds just like the word alive. Christians view three as God's number, probably because of the Trinity, but maybe because of the three crosses on Golgotha.

And, of course, you've probably used the phrase third time's the charm, or third time lucky on numerous occasions, meaning you're bound to get it right on the third try. You never hear anyone saying, tenth time's the charm, because if it takes ten times to get something right, then you probably shouldn't be trying it anyway.

As you can see, ten is a number of convenience. It's more a placeholder than it is an actual source of information. Ten is a nice safe grouping, even if we're not able to access every part of that grouping. It's just too much.

But the Law of Thirds plays an important role in the many tens of our lives. Our brains acknowledge the lists and subdivisions of the number ten and even celebrates them. But when it comes to using the information, give the brain a nice solid group of three and suddenly everyone is impressed.

Eleven, Twelve and MORE

An 11-sided polygon is called a hendecagon. It is one of the least stable shapes you can make. A three sided polygon is called a triangle. It is, on the other hand, perhaps the most stable of all shapes.

There are 11 players on an American football team. There are 11 players on an English football team, even though there is little similarity between the two games. Soccer is apparently the most sophisticated game because it only requires three officials.

Twelve goes under the curious and less-than-exact term dozen. Thirteen somewhere along the line got the reputation of being unlucky and now everyone avoids it like the plague.

The 13th floor of almost any apartment house is nearly impossible to lease and some builders have been known to skip the number altogether. It is so unpopular with hotel guests that many proprietors simply use the 13th floor to house all the ventilation equipment and all power distribution machinery. Talk about a lack of respect.

And how about a dinner party with 13 people sitting around the table? I don't think so! Pull up another chair and add a child's teddy bear.

You remember Woodrow Wilson's famous fourteen points. These were the magical points that Wilson used to ensure the US people and the US congress that World War I actually served more of a purpose than just putting the Germans in their place. The fourteen points were also to serve as the basis for surrender of the German Army once the war ended in 1918. Each point turned out to a be a 'stand alone' point meant to appease any number of different supporters, so, as it turned out, almost none of the points had any relevance to the previous one.

However, the Law of Thirds once again came into play in this case, because no one of sound mind is going to focus on 14 of anything, much less 14 points of war. In the end, Wilson took his own domestic policy and used it to sum up the most vital three areas that he hoped would be a recipe for peace. They were:

- Free trade
- Democracy
- Self-determination.

Now those were three things people could understand and hang their hats on. Good politics on Wilson's part that also showed his understanding of how the human brain best functioned. On a historical note, the fourteen points had very little to do with the Treaty of Versailles that eventually ended the war. The treaty was built around 35 points broken into seven sections, and everyone probably signed it because it was so incomprehensible and not worthy of debating. Of course, that's just speculation on my part.

There are, some say, 15 causes of color, from organic compounds and vibrations, to pure semiconductors, interferences and refraction. But there are others who say, in fact, there are only three causes of color:

- Light is <u>made</u> in the yellow glow of the candle
- Light is <u>lost</u> when sunlight filters through stained glass
- Light is <u>moved</u> when sky turns a crimson sunset.

The reason is straightforward: color can only be made, lost, or moved.

How about this one! There are 16 personality types, from serious and quiet to assertive and outspoken. But the truth is an employer only wants to know three things when he or she is considering a new hire: will you lead, follow, or best be left to work alone.

And then there are the 17 Zurich Axioms. These bits of sound and savory advice were formulated in an attempt by a number of Swiss bankers living in New York City to advise everyone who wasn't a Swiss banker on how to best invest our savings. Thank you very much.

The list, first and foremost, is far too long for any person of right mind to employ, but it is also madly diverse. It covers such odd subjects as when and when not to put down roots, which medium of clairvoyance to trust and which to avoid, which hunches to play and which not. How about this: sell too soon is a wise man's motto. Or: when the ship begins to sink, don't think, jump. How anyone is supposed to take on board so many rules and ideas and meld them into one coherent investment strategy is beyond me. I'm sure the world's most powerful computers would struggle to process so many rules with such an array of obscurity. How about these three elementary rules of investment to sum it up:

- Let time work for you
- Never throw good money after bad
- Do your homework.

Simple, to the point, and hard to refute.

Did you know there are 18 distinct penguin species? But most of us are only familiar with those that are: mostly black, mostly white, and the ones with yellow feathers on their heads. Yes, the Law of Thirds even dictates how we qualify our penguins.

How about a list of 19? If you travel back to 1692 when King Charles I was the ruler of all England, apparently the House of Lords and the House of Commons got together because they were feeling like the King was acting more like a dictator than a monarch and put together a list of demands that would give them more of a say in how things were done. So arose the Nineteen Propositions. We won't go into the list per se, but it is safe to say that it included a lot of you must do this and you must accept that. You can imagine how poorly these went over with the King. He, naturally, rejected the list, and the country descended into civil war. If the Lords and Commons had been smart, they would have simplified things according to the Law of Thirds, saying in effect:

- Lords and Commons must now approval all the King's appointments
- Lords and Commons will now control the army and the militia

- The King will stay in his castle from now on and avoid the floor of Parliament at all costs.

Sure, the end result would have still been civil war, but at least the reasons would have been crystal clear.

The bottom line is this. Whether you're a king making grand proclamations or a house wife fixing a to-do list to the refrigerator, it is wise to remember that grand lists of any kind can be immensely daunting things.

One of the advantages of the 'fridge-list' is that when you add an item, you become relieved of some of the burden of seeing the item done. I'm sure the parliamentarians in the time of King Charles were patting themselves on the back as soon as their list was done and thinking the job was half done simply by airing the list for all to see. Not that it worked out that way.

Creating your ubiquitous list of things to do – and how often do these things come across as demands – might appear to relieve you of your burden, but it may very well induce an emetic reaction, just like it probably did with the king. The natural reaction is to reject first, vomit second and fight back like a rat in a corner third. A nice list of three.

When using a list, ensure it's arranged as a contract. Think of the advantages and note how nicely the three elements fit the natural approach of even the most stubborn brain:

- Give
- Take
- Scope.

That way, it doesn't appear that you're making demands, but rather creating a working arrangement. It also appears that you're getting twice back for what you're putting in, and who can argue with that. What's more, the contract model also gives you the opportunity to disguise some of the things on the list with a blatant discount of some kind, or more effective, something out-and-out free. Now you're really making your to-do list sound appealing.

Balance is the key. And nothing demonstrates balance than an easily understood list of three. That is a point we need to make whether the list is two, four, fourteen, or twenty-four. Balance is always the key and our brains naturally gravitate to the comfortable, yet stimulating balance of the Law of Thirds.

There are twenty amino acids, from lysine (lys), glycine (gln) to valine (val) and serine (ser). Notice anything familiar about these? That's right. All amino acids are designated by three letter codes known and recognized throughout the scientific world. And what's more, all amino acids are built from three distinct parts: an amine, an acid and a side chain. Hail the Law of Thirds.

We revisit the contracts of war (or the succession of war) with Japan's 21 Demands put to Yuan Shikai, the President of the Republic of China, following the second Sino-Japanese War. The demands were placed into five sub-groupings, but it was the third group that was of particular interest to Japan, giving them control of something called the Hanyeping mining and metallurgical complex and known to be extremely valuable. After much to-ing and fro-ing, the Chinese agreed to 14 of the demands, but the terms of the third group were not brought to bear. Ultimately the demands were annulled in the Washington conference of 1921-22 and sovereignty returned to the Chinese.

There are 23 auxiliary verbs in the English language, from could, would and should to may, might and must. And all of them have appeared in this confusing but varied chapter on numerical division, but the three most important are those that promote taking action will, can and do.

Twenty Four

Twenty-four deserves its own chapter.

There are, of course, 24 hours in every day, which is the lodestar for almost every activity on the planet, from growing cycles to sleeping cycles.

Rest assured that it's no accident that the day itself is defined according to day-month-year, and is nicely divided into three time periods of eight hours each. Our brains require it, and we are most efficient when we stay on this eight hour track. It might be generalizing to say that we work for eight hours, allot eight hours for sleep and save eight hours for what we might call 'self' time or 'transition' time. This the time that allows us to maximize our eight hours at work and to prepare ourselves for eight hours of sleep. Messing with the brain's internal clock is always precarious, and the most obvious signs are three in number:

- We're less efficient
- We're more irritable
- We're more forgetful.

Plants are no different from people when it comes to the 24 hour day. Plants also carve these hours into three cycles.

- Absorbing light
- Absorbing water
- Hibernating.

And then we have the fascinating, magnificently crafted timepieces that track in the most precise way our most important 24 hour day.

Picture the face of a watch or that of a clock. They communicate in three ways: visually, kinetically and aesthetically.

It is the face of the clock that communicates the time through our eyes and into our brains. Why is this important to our discussion of the Law of Thirds? Because a watch is designed and equipped with three hands:

- The hour hand
- The minute hand
- The second hand.

It's perfectly efficient while treating our brains to their desired aesthetic.

Look further in the face of a beautiful timepiece. Note that each quarter of an hour is split into three perfectly symmetrical periods of five minutes. Also note that very often a watch or clock has been designed without the three five-minute subdivisions, but it is no coincidence that our brains happily interpolate these missing timeframes.

On the other hand, our brains naturally find a watch face set only with markings denoting the 12 o'clock hour and the 6 o'clock hour to be grating, lacking an aesthetic component and just plain dysfunctional. Please note this painful series of three.

Most watches, my own included, are graced with three icons: the hands, the numerals and the lettering. It is also no accident the lettering that incorporates the name of the manufacturer and the model makes use of three fonts in three different sizes. As I said, this is no accident.

After all, the watch face is one of the most studied and perfected things ever invented in terms of style, ergonomics and aesthetics. Yes, another tribute to the Law of Thirds.

Want one more? How about the fact that watch faces that incorporate roman numerals into their design rely on exactly three numerals: I, V and X.

Take King Louis XIV, the enigmatic King of France from 1638 to 1715. In one of his many famous, if oddly conceived mandates, he instructed clock makers throughout his kingdom to produce dials with a 'IIII' rather than a 'IV,' begging the question: Why in the world would he have done that? Simple. So the dial had a three way rotational symmetry, with IIII balancing the XII and VIII at 12 and 8! Voila!

Observe the crookedness of the face as the numeral III tries to balance the VIII and IX.

Our natural thought process also breaks up the 24 hours of our day into three easily remembered cycles: morning, afternoon and night.

The twenty-fourth law of power tells us to play the perfect courtier, which requires us to perfect the art of flattery while concealing your true intentions, which, of course, is the Third Law of Power.

And finally, from time to music, we find there are twenty-four major and minor keys in western music, but that the most important and lasting measure of tonality in music is created by major and minor chords based upon three notes. This triad — meaning built from three, such as the G, B and D notes that form a standard G-Major chord — have been at the heart of music created by everyone from Bach and Mozart to Dylan and the Beatles. And if that doesn't say something about the power of the Law of Thirds, I don't know what does.

A Law of Thirds Interlude

From two to 24, we've explored the intricacies of dividing thoughts and ideas, events and situations, people, places and all things into categories and subdivisions that invariably have more staying power and relevance when the Law of Thirds intervenes and our natural thought processes are allowed to function the way our brains know they should.

Lists are nothing more than a representation of our thoughts, but please don't draw the erroneous conclusion that employing thirds in the natural thought process suggests something you can easily describe using three bullet points. Not true, as this section will demonstrate. The conclusions that can and do emerge from the Law of Thirds are many and varied, yet they are always logical and pragmatic.

Remember also that these words of wisdom in themselves are very powerful, and can be used in your everyday life, but they all stem from understanding how our brains and the brains of our fellow man function.

The Law of Thirds provides a natural paradigm that fits our memories, stimulates our power of recall, and provides the intellect with the most effective tools possible. We're smarter, more entertaining, more literary, more athletic and more artistic when we tap the Law of Thirds.

The mind works naturally with the Law of Thirds, but you and I still have to be willing to accept the concept and know that it fits our most natural thought processes. The most important technique we can implement in distilling multiple points into hierarchical relations of three is to recognize that the Law of Thirds is neither man-made nor manipulative; it is the way our brains work when we're not forcing the issue or trying too hard. Let it be, as the Beatles once sang, and the lyric could well be the perfect anthem for the Law of Thirds at its best.

The larger the list or the subdivision, the more dedicated our brains are to reducing them to manageable, useful, inspiring lists of three. We visited such iconic areas as the Ten Commandments of the Christian bible and the eight planets of our solar system, and discovered that most of us distill even these universal truths down in ways that emphasize the power of three and the thought process that finds them most natural.

It's not confusion that drives the brain to restore the order of threes, but rather an innate understanding that three is the number of power, the number of learning, the number of listening and the number of processing at its most effective level. And what a relief it is to know that we've been born with these often overlooked gifts.

The Law of Thirds, as we saw in our earlier discussions, is timeless. It can be traced back many centuries. It is a constant in the thought process of man even as our technologies change and our problems become more complex. The brain simplifies when it needs to, and it pushes us when a good push is in order, but it always relies on the Law of Thirds to generate thought at its highest, most efficient level.

In the following sections, we look at divisions, classifications and groups that are commonly ordered according to the Law of Thirds. We will pay close attention to the how and the why, but we will also look closely at cause and effect, because the more aware we are of this natural thought process the more it becomes, well, natural.

We will also travel deeper into the philosophical aspects of the Law of Thirds, gaining along the way a viable understanding for how thirds can be applied to ideas, concepts and observations.

Finally, we will explore how these groups and subdivisions, ideas and concepts are actually constructed via our thoughts, even applying thirds on top of thirds and compounding the power of the principle on multiple levels.

Hang on for the ride.

Einstein's Theory

Make something that is obvious to you a relationship between two things that the person you are communicating to understands.

When Stephen Hawking, perhaps the world's best-known physicist, wrote his everyman masterpiece called A Brief History of Time, he was advised that his book sales would be inversely proportional to the number of equations included in the text. In other words, if you're writing a book for the layman, go sparingly on the science equations if you don't want to lose your readers. So I guess it's good to know that even so-called proven equations are not without their risks.

Equations to scientists are like number one records to singers; it is a way to be remembered in history, a way to establish your legacy, and a sure way to have your name forever cursed by students in every science classroom from L.A. to Liverpool. More important than climbing a mountain or discovering a new species, equations have stature abounding fame and respect.

Scientific equations are just like mountains and hit records; some are higher and more dangerous to climb; some get played more often on the radio, are re-recorded by other singers, and are hummed in the shower. If you want to get your scientific equation onto the A-List, it needs to describe the interaction of three variables.

The simplest equations are expressed as three definable parts: x + y = z.

A simple equation such as 3 + 4 is easily answered with a glance and a word: 3 + 4 = 7. Just say it. Yet make the equation just slightly more complicated, say 3 + 8 + 2. In this case, we can't do it without breaking it down. First, we calculate 3 + 8 = 11. Then we add 2 to the 11 and hey presto, it's lucky old 13. Don't worry, that's as difficult as this book gets, but I hope the point is proven.

But what do equations mean? Underneath them we have equality and relationships. The equality is what the scientist knows to be true. The hunch played out in a laboratory or dreamt up under an apple tree. The relationship is the way it is communicated to others.

From Newton to Boyle classical physics produced many hit records. Einstein in his equation $E = MC^2$ linked energy to matter. Einstein wanted to tell the world that matter IS energy, the two things are one and the same. Matter is nothing more than energy twisted up into sub-atomic particles, but what Einstein's equation does is link our perceptions of what is matter and what is energy. Newton famed for the discovery of gravity, really introduced the concept of mass to link gravitational force and the accelerating apple.

So, now for the conclusion: for effective communication express your ideas using the relationship of two things familiar to the person you're communicating with. If you do this, their mind evaluates the equation subconciously. Well, that's the theory at least. Let us look at how it works in the real world.

Let's talk about the three traits of identity: gender, race and social class. We have fallen into the trap of using these traits to pigeonhole people, whether it's intentional or not. Although this is meant to be a rather light-hearted example, relationship based thinking can and should be used for more sensitive topics such as identity. In both America and Europe, people with black skin were commonly called 'Negro', which literally means 'black' in Portuguese. This term was used as a moniker for identity going back as far as the slave trade in the fifteenth century and became a term of significance during the civil rights movement of the 1950s and beyond. Various different monikers were also attempted as a means of identifying this 'racial' group, yet each one just seemed to offend as much as the next. Why is that? The answer: nobody likes being identified by any name except their own; that's universal. Race, gender, and social class all rely on monikers. Is it any wonder the system doesn't work?

These days, we're attempting to rectify the situation by switching to a relationship-based conversation that we hope promotes understanding, equality and acceptance. The three traits of an evolving society. And yes, we have a long way to go.

Nonetheless, we have in this day and age turned to the term 'African American' to describe people with black skin, even if many people who fall under this label can trace their ancestry to many other parts of the world other than Africa. Yet, there is a positive here, and that is the relationship between ancestral origins and citizenship, and these two things are easy to understand. This relationship-based approach has a definite downside, however, and that is its unfortunate application to an entire population of people. We now have the 'Mexican American' group, the 'Spanish American' group, the 'Irish American' group and of course the 'Native American' group. You just have to wonder when Americans with ethnic ties to Europe will begin insisting that the 'white' moniker is dropped altogether. Just think of a world where labels no longer exist, and the color of a person's skin has nothing to do with their identity.

And speaking of identity, we should talk here about the issue facing children. There are three key questions to ask this very dicey, yet undeniably important problem. Where does their identity come from? Who do they belong to? What defines their relationship when it comes to adults?

To a person looking in, the identity is undeniably clear: a chip off the old block, like father like son. The very same DNA makes them the very same person. As for the question of belonging, that would seem easy enough to answer as long as the child in question is a minor. But is it really? Belonging is defined by three indisputable desires: being connected, being acknowledged and being given an equal footing.

When an adult introduces himself or herself to a child, addressing the issue of identity is vastly important. Do you say, "Are you one of good William's brood?" Or would it be more appropriate to say, "I know your father. William's very proud of you. He says you think for yourself." Small difference? Hardly. The first suggests an identity based upon ownership – something that they are. The second implies an identity based upon self – something they have. Pretty significant, don't you think?

Should a manager be "proud of my team" or "proud to be a part of the team?" The former statement suggests ownership; the latter statement suggests a relationship. No difference for the manager, perhaps, a world of difference to the team members listening.

Picture yourself talking with a child who's not doing particularly well in class. There are three goals. The first is to state a positive, i.e. "We're glad to see that you're making an effort." The second is to state the problem, i.e. "Your grades are not going to allow you to move on to the next grade." The third is to wipe the slate clean, i.e. "We're going to work together to right the ship."

It's probably not very effective to say, "You're acting like a dropout." Instead, it's better to talk about performance from a relationship standpoint, saying, "Students who don't study are bound to get low grades." This targets the relationship between studying and grades rather than painting a dreary picture of what he or she is fast becoming; in this case, a dropout. State a positive, get to the problem, clean the slate and move on. Thirds; there's no better way to communicate.

Relationship-based thinking is not the preserve of physicists and psychologists. Advertisers love to use relationship-based concepts in their campaigns. A favorite of mine is from the police on the subject of driving with a cell phone. The police know that driving with a cell phone equals accidents and sometimes death. So the advertising campaign is built around the relationship between the two, stating, "Meet your police officer – the grim reaper." Behaving like children, adult drivers don't like direct commands such as, "Don't use your cell phone when driving," so by focusing on the relationship between the action and death, we are more open to receiving and accepting the message.

Try this one for size. When you're talking to your partner and trying to make a point of the importance of your personal relationship, you can see how effective it is when you juxtapose two variables that together paint a vivid picture: "You mean everything to me," or, "Before you, my life was nothing." Talk about scoring some points with your significant other!

Einstein's theory of creating an obvious conclusion by demonstrating the working relationship of two variables reinforces at a visceral level how our natural thought process best expresses itself using thirds and more thirds.

The message? Make it a part of your daily life and be amazed.

Mantras

To defend against probing questions, audits and attacks, form three lines of defense and make sure everyone knows what they are.

Einstein described himself as a militant pacifist, and in that same breath came up with the mantra-like manifesto "fighting for peace". Was that oxymoronic, or perhaps he knew which way the joke was really going?

Mantras do of course have their origins in religion. From the not so profound or eloquent Om of transcendental meditation, to Hinduism lending us the more familiar Hare Krishna mantra, the mantra itself is just four lines, sixteen words in total. Let's give it a go:

> *Hare Krishna Hare Krishna*
> *Krishna Krishna Hare Hare*
> *Hare Rama Hare Rama*
> *Rama Rama Hare Hare.*

Notice anything? There are just three unique words used. Notice anything wrong with it? Well I guess the answer is no, but that's the whole point. Mantras are ultra-defensive phrases. They do not invite questioning or conversation. A literary non-stick coating. From Om to the devotees of the god Vishnu, the mantra is recited to achieve internal peace and transformation and don't make for topical discussion.

Mantras are not of course purely the preserve of religion. From politics to business, the defensive aspects of mantras are an oft used technique to block dialog during a conversation. Let's progress to an example from a trade union leader. "We want negotiation without confrontation or intimidation." This little gem of a mantra is attributed to Tony Woodley, UK Airline Union's General Secretary during the 2010 British Airways cabin crew strike. He went on, "Only negotiation, not intimidation or litigation can keep British Airways flying." You see the trend. In fact, six months on, he was still playing the same card when speaking to the media. This type of mantra although used defensively has a more slogan like feel to express beliefs.

For a truly conversation blocking mantra we can look to the British Army stationed in Afghanistan. Their mantra is "Take, hold, build", and it is has proved so powerful that few oppose or question the logic. And if any less-than-committed soldier was to ask the question, "What are we doing here?" you can rest assured that his comrades will give him their own interpretation of the mantra. Compare this mantra with the centuries old principles of war - Warfare has three main objectives:

1. To conquer and destory the armed power of the enemy
2. To take possession of his material and other sources of strength
3. To gain public opinion.

If it all works the way it is supposed to, the mantra becomes ingrained in the subconscious mind and eventually forms the basis for conscious thinking.

The most effective mantras, not surprisingly, are three word idioms. Take perhaps the most famous one in recent memory, Nike's iconic: Just Do It. This may be Nike's most famous calling card, but it is not their first three word mantra. Previously, they marketed their cache of shoes, clothes, and equipment – yes, another three-headed monster – using the mantra: Authentic Athletic Performance. Not the showstopper that Just Do It is, but not bad.

The three word mantra has a ring to it that our natural thought process is logically attracted to. It is also not surprising that our brains respond to the use of three words in a more forthright way than it would a two or four-line phrase. It has more power and triggers more feedback.

"Do It Now" and "Go for it" are two other common mantras we often hear spouted in the business world, though I'm not sure they don't sound more like clichés than slogans. They do work just the same, "Better do it now than wish it done", is I believe the extended version, and we shouldn't be afraid to use them for the purpose for which they were intended. Just don't go turning them into a religion.

Sony has "It's a Sony", Coca Cola has "Coke Is It." McDonald's has "I'm Lovin' It." And Disney has "Fun Family Entertainment."

The problem is, these mantras all strike me as lofty, defensive, or archaic. Come on! Are you saying Disney can't come up with something more evocative than "Fun Family Entertainment?" It sounds boring, tiresome and uninspiring to me. But did you notice something? Disney's mantra survived my three word assault – of course I only attacked the 'fun' aspect. The other two words (family and entertainment) held out and supported the mantra.

Click to Buy, Buy it now, Sale now on, reduced to clear. Clearly the retail face of capitalism is not immune to the power. I guess they have nothing to lose, huh?

So how do we fight against the onslaught of mantras filling the airwaves and shouting down at us from billboards? You fight fire with fire. You take away the mantra's power. You use the Law of Thirds to your advantage. You rework the mantra in your mind with something less powerful, something more ironic, or something downright insulting.

It was Sony, Coke is not, Not Lovin' That or, Don't Do it. Okay, so those aren't the best examples, but you get the idea. Fight fire with fire.

The defense component is a strong element of the mantra, both pro and con. A mantra can give us strength, God bless America, but it can also sap us of our strength, one more time. A mantra can give us focus, but it can also divert our focus. A mantra counters the negative effects of a world filled with negatives, but a mantra can also be a negative.

But just as a mantra can be used to control our thoughts or influence our buying habits, a mantra can also be a powerful tool. A mantra can spur you into action, i.e. make a difference. A mantra can positively affect your self-esteem, i.e. just be yourself. And a mantra can help you find peace, i.e. Trust in God.

In the last section we went from science to words, now we go from words to science, this time it's the human body, and the biology of its three lines of defense. And for those of us who aren't exactly sure what they are, have a look:

1. Our outer shell, meaning our skin and mucous membranes, and those other protective 'organs' such as hair, nails, sweat glands and oil glands
2. Our innate immune system, what causes our skin to go red when we scratch it; our heart, arteries, veins, capillaries and blood
3. Our adaptive immune system, white blood cells and such like, our bone marrow, our spleen, our tonsils, our lymph nodes.

After disease and infection, the most common cause of death in the western world is traffic accidents. It should be no surprise that there are three lines of defense in the prevention of them.

1. Traffic management. How the roads themselves interact with other road users. The design and operation of lighting, signs, roundabouts and slipways
2. Driver training. Teaching the drivers necessary skills to behave in an orderly and safe manner, not speeding, not driving drunk etc
3. The final layer is left to the driver adapting to the shortcomings of other people on the roads, whether they be pedestrians or other drivers.

Both examples of human biology and road accident prevention are vertical defense strategies, each layer sitting behind the next.

Even attacking words can be made into defensive mantras. It is indeed said that the best form of defense is attack. "We will fight" has to be said in a fairly belligerent way to be interpreted as a defense. Yet this mantra was a favorite of Britain's greatest wartime politician, Winston Churchill.

> *We will fight* on the beaches
> *We will fight* on the landing grounds
> *We will fight* on the streets.

As the speech goes on, the defensive tone is increased. The mantra cannot be attacked; the mantra is impermeable. The mantra is drummed into the brain, to the point of numbing your neurons like a knuckle rubbed onto one's skull. It is unanswerable.

Repetition is an important rhetorical device. Churchill's "We will fight" is used here as what's known in linguistic circles as an anaphora – that is, the same phrase occurring at the beginning of each line.

A mantra doesn't need to be constructed from words. All around us we see corporate logos, styling and branding that is defensive – instilling a sense of trust with the consumer. Mantras can also be actions, driving instructors teach us to mirror, signal and maneuver as the defensive way to behave when taking to the road.

Every man, woman and child should have a mantra. And the most effective mantras throughout history have paid tribute, knowingly or not, to the Law of Thirds. Why? Because that's the way we think. Those are the mantras that have proved most effective and most lasting. Start a cult. Get one for yourself.

Three Letter Acronyms (TLAs)

You should focus and concentrate on implementing and perfecting the idea. Let the masses come up with colloquialisms for your invention.

If people are going to distill your name, brand or concept, ensure it means something, make sure it cannot be misunderstood.

The problem with a two letter acronym is that it gets lost in the shuffle. Two letter acronyms can be effective if you're trying to identify a state (CA = California or NY = New York) or even a nation (UK = United Kingdom), but if you're trying to create an unforgettable brand for yourself and your company, the three letter acronym is unsurpassed.

"You can sum up my strategy in three letters. N-H-S." Those were the words of David Cameron, Britain's would be Prime Minister, during the Conservative Party's spring conference in preface to the elections there in 2010. If you're British, you know that NHS stands for National Healthcare System. If you're not, you'll understand that Cameron's devotion to that three letter acronym got him elected.

Three letter acronyms are ubiquitous; a longer acronym is often a neologism that coins a new word rather than creates a firestorm. Take RADAR, for example, which stands for Radio Detection and Ranging. But, alas, it didn't start out that way. You see, the military is very fond of its acronyms, and it was the British acronym RDF – which stands for Range and Detection Finding – that won the day originally. Apparently, the Americans didn't like the name or the acronym, and it was reborn as RADAR.

Needless to say, it didn't take the Germans long to get into the game when they shot down and captured a British RAF bomber carrying H2S radar. H2S, a really nifty three letter acronym, stands for hydrogen sulfide, a colorless, very poisonous, and really foul smelling substance. H2S radar was the first ground mapping radar to be used in combat and for night bombing, and the Germans were dying to get their hands on it. What they did was to reassemble the radar unit they captured that fateful day and used the technology to develop their own three letter acronym – NRD – which stood for Naxos Radar Detector. That evened things out; now everyone could drop their bombs at night.

Some companies are better known for their three letter acronym than they are their actual name. IBM is rarely referred to as International Business Machines. NEC has not been called the Nippon Electric Company in years. UAL is the thinking man and woman's choice for United Airlines.

What about the most powerful intelligence and police agencies in the world? Few people call the Central Intelligence Agency anything other than the CIA. Ask ten people what FBI stands for and less than half will say Federal Bureau of Investigation, but they all know the FBI is something you don't want to mess around with.

What about sports? The MLB stands for Major League Baseball. The NFL is a worldwide brand that most people recognize as the National Football League. In Australia, they have the NRL, or National Rugby League. In Scotland, we have the SPL, or Scottish Premier League.

Does SAP stand for Soon as Possible, Strategic Action Plan, or Solar Array Paddle? See A Problem? SAP stands for the computer database vendor who markets Systems, Applications, and Products, but appears to have no real name other than SAP, or should that be S.A.P (ess-ay-pee)? So there is the very real fear of a breakdown of communication (BOC), where neither side quite understands what the other side is talking about, each referring to the other as OTL (Out to Lunch). Or is that Off the List?

WWW has become perhaps the best known TLA on the planet, most often seen in an internet address line such as www.three-letter-acronym.com. Ironically, there are still an extraordinary number of people who don't know that "www" stands for World Wide Web, which is a system of interlinked hypertext documents we now just call the Web. And why is that? Maybe because it takes us longer to say out the acronym than what it stands for! The acronym dubleya-dubleya-dubleya is a massive nine syllables. Is it any wonder most websites work all the same without the www prefix?

Of course acronyms are not limited to just words; there are numbers and symbols a plenty. This is a great piece of out-of-the-box thinking that is directly correlated with our natural thinking process and the rules of the Law of Thirds. Out of the box, and yet not so out of the box.

BMW (Bayerische Motoren Werke) uses three numeral model names for the majority of the cars they produce. The first number relates to the size of the chassis. The second and third numbers relate to the engine's capacity. Thus a BMW 750 is a limousine chassis with a 5.0 liter engine, a very nice car. Whereas a BMW 323 is a compact executive car with a 2.3 liter engine, also a pretty nice car.

Sometimes more abstract numerical concepts are used for branding, and sometimes they just leave you scratching your head. Let's use Intel as an example. Intel is a major manufacturer of microprocessors and a name most of us are familiar with. In 1978, it launched a chip to compete with the popular Z80 (the Z80 corresponding to Zilog '80, where 80 is a truncation of 8080) called the 8086. Confused? So am I. The 8086 proved a popular platform for DOS, a very early Microsoft software package. Intel went on to launch 80186 and 80286. The 80286 became hugely popular and was colloquially known as a 286.

I shouldn't need to remind you of what happened next, but I will just in case. The 386 came along, then the 486. Things were really hopping when the subject of trademarks came into play, and a high court ruled that numbers could not be trademarked. This put the kibosh on Intel's numbering system, so they switched to Pentium.

Boeing is another major company with now famous three numbered model names. We all know their 700-series, ranging from the 707 to the 787. Of course it was never intended for the number to mean so much as it does in today's airline lexicon. The first Boeing plane was known as the B & W Seaplane. In 1928, they launched a bi-plane called the P-12, but not surprisingly it also went by the TLA of F4B. Oh, and yes, they produced exactly 528 of this design. What does all this prove? It proves that a series of three is nature's most effective way of jogging our memories.

In the 1930s, Boeing's passenger planes were called things like the Stratoliner and Stratocruiser. You never saw a three number acronym. But just like Intel, the 7x7 series changed everything, and the 707 hailed in a new age for the jet plane and a brand that almost everyone could identify.

So the question is, does giving your product a TLA make you an instant success? Of course the answer is no. But don't ever lose sight of the fact that our brains gobble up information of any kind presented in thirds, so branding based upon this premise is not to be taken lightly.

As we saw in earlier sections, thirds is very often the result of collective reasoning. Someone says something off-the-cuff, and it has a ring to it. The name, the word, the sound, yes, and the acronym sticks in the individuals' conscious and manifests in the collective consciousness.

Trying to second-guess the power of collective thought just won't work? Trying to second-guess the very process that comes naturally to the brain (I'm talking about your brain BTW) just won't work either. You're just as likely to get lucky on an 888.com gambling site. And what are those odds? Not good.

Currency

Where one value mechanism spans disparate sections, consider changes to the perception of value so that a segregation and insulation emerges.

Money has many origins, from the cowrie shell and the chicken to beads and barley. Money is fundamental to trade – unless you prefer bartering or gifting – and is required to be fungible; that is, to have a value locally as well as nationally and internationally.

One of the problems with the cowrie shell – or anything that is affected by supply and availability – is that it is a more valuable currency where cowrie shells are rare and less so, of course, where cowrie shells are abundant. You don't need a cowrie shell if they're washing up on the beach outside your house by the hundreds.

This section, however, is not just about money. It's about what we perceive as currency in general. We wouldn't wish to repay a favor with a $20 bill (well, some of you might). A bouquet of flowers or a bottle of wine are almost always a more appropriate way of saying thank you than opening your wallet. Or, if I happened to be the one doing you a favor – chocolates please!

Flowers, wine and chocolate as forms of currency? Absolutely!

How about the time we spend with our children? When expressed in terms of currency, how valuable is that to us? Extremely. And how valuable is it to our kids? Would they prefer to trade in this one-on-one time for a new bicycle? In some cases, much to the chagrin of you and I as parents, the answer is yes. Still, however, a currency by any other name, is it not?

Here's a tough one. How about the decision we sometimes make to sacrifice our time at home for time in the office? In terms of dollars and cents and putting food on the table, it's a simple choice. But the sacrifice and the loss of quality time at home is a type of currency as well, and we have to make our decisions wisely in cases like this or the well containing the currency of self-actualization may well run dry. And no currency is worth that.

Let's begin further discussions, however, with a financial focus on the three types of money: accumulated money, lifestyle money and transferred money. Or, what you save, what you spend and what you give away. And correspondingly so, let's remind ourselves that wealth lasts just three generations: the first generation works hard and accumulates wealth; the second preserves it out of fear; whilst the third spends, spends, spends. Did you notice? Exactly three spends. No less, no more.

Nature, as we all know, has long provided us with its own brand of currency. For example, base metals like nickel, zinc, copper and lead have always been a type of marginal currency. But they possess three real value assets that contribute to their use. One, they're worth something because they can be used for purposes far and wide, like building and construction. Two, they can also be difficult to extract from the ground, adding to their value. Third, they have the advantage of being fairly easy to mint, if, for example, you decide to create a currency that can cross borders or travel from kingdom to kingdom.

What about precious metals like gold, silver, platinum and palladium? In this case, these metals possess three intrinsic qualities. One, they are fairly rare. Two, they are hard to find. Three, they have perceived value, which, of course, is priceless.

Let's look a little deeper now at the medium of the exchange process. One of the first things we discover is that it is no accident at all that there are three types of metal most often used throughout history as currency of some type.

Gold – the currency of bankers; also the currency of snobs – has historically been used to support the issuance of banknotes. Gold coins issued to the general public were, and still are, objects of allure that are now a favorite of coin collectors and coin hoarders, which is probably why you find them tucked away in a safe somewhere rather than popping up in the grocery store or at your local bingo game. Gold is the metal of kings, from Darius to Tushratta and has been at the heart of 100 wars throughout the course of time.

Silver – the currency of merchants and trade; also the currency of gentlemen – was historically a favorite form of exchange in the international markets of everything from tea and silk to camels and goats. Its use as a currency can be traced back as far 700 BC when the Lydians of Asia Minor bartered the metal for goods all around the areas we now call the Middle East and the Mediterranean. Smart folks! Silver dollars, a favorite among coin aficionados, have for many years acted as a circulating currency with Mexican, American and European issues, all now highly prized. The Chinese absolutely loved silver dollars; it must have been the weight and the size that appealed to them, a sort of security blanket amongst the hordes. But Lavere Redfield, a turn of the century investor, took it to a new level by hoarding four hundred thousand silver dollars and never spending one; or so the story goes.

Copper – the currency of barter; also the currency of the people – is nowadays used in producing the smallest of coins, a red cent as some call the penny, and, by all accounts, nearly worthless. Historically, you could get drunk for a penny – and dead drunk for two.

Useful in making transactions at the local tavern or inn, the apothecary next door, at the neighborhood blacksmith, and, of course, in houses of ill-repute far and wide.

Banknotes have been around longer than you might think. The Chinese were known to use them in the seventh century, if not earlier. In the west, paper money took a little longer to catch on and only hit the big time in the last hundred years or so.

Banknotes now represent the most important form of currency or means of exchange in our worldwide society. There are three indisputable reasons why banknotes have become a primary source of exchange. For purposes of foreign exchange, nothing is more fungible. When it comes to cost, nothing is cheaper to make. When it comes to ease of use, nothing can beat it.

So what's been happening recently? Sure we still carry our wallets and purses and most of them have a few dollars and a few coins in them, but the days of giving something tangible – a coin or a chicken or a crisp dollar bill – for something equally as tangible in return – a visit from the doctor or vegetables from the market – has given way to a new economy, one based upon debt, in particular the ubiquitous credit card.

One George Clanson calls debt the "currency of slaves", and if that's not food for thought, I don't know what is. It is a case, I suppose, of too many people hoping to get something for nothing and finding themselves buried in debt. Sounds like most of the governments of the world, doesn't it?

However, the Law of Thirds still plays its hand. Consider these three pieces of evidence proving the depth of the debt crisis:

1. The percentage of disposable income used to make debt payments is now near an all-time high.
2. The number of bankruptcies keeps setting records
3. Foreclosures are at modern highs, and the number of home loans more than 30 days overdue is rising.

Our brains don't need further evidence than this of the crisis at hand. Our brains see this crisis presented using three stark statistics, and it's all we need to understand our plight. Less than three and we might not take it as seriously. More than three and we might be overwhelmed and ignore the problem.

But let's take it further. A debt-based economy and the currency we use to facilitate it are split into the three discernable sectors: banking, trade and retail.

The banking sector uses loans and mortgages to foster interest-bearing debt, funding everything from car and house loans to business and school loans. The banks increase their capital base by collecting deposits – that, ironically, the government insures – and upon which they pay minimal interest. It's a real racket, and it makes you think we should all be bankers.

The trade sector is to a very great degree also debt-based. Almost no one actually pays for shipments of goods upon receipt of them. Not at all. Companies big and small agree upon placing an order to pay for said goods within some set period of time, normally somewhere between ten days and six months. You've heard the term Net-30. This indicates a contract to pay within 30 days. But it's still debt no matter how you paint the picture.

The retail sector, once the domain of paper money and cash sales, is now ruled by the use of credit cards, and people like you and me charge everything from motorboats to café lattes on our precious little cards, willing to absorb usurious interest payments. The result is a society up to its neck in debt and staying afloat by making minimum monthly payments.

But what about this thing we call government debt? How does the Law of Thirds play into that? Try this simple equation on for size (damn, there goes my book sales again).

$$3^{3^3}$$

In math speak, that's three raised to the power three raised to the power three. And what's the result? 7.6 trillion!!! Still don't get it? $7.6 trillion is the total outstanding US Government debt. How's that for coincidences. Or is it really a coincidence at all?

Have no doubts, debt is currency, just as surely as a silver dollar, a penny, or a banknote.

But let's get a little more obscure here and take a peek at the airline industry. What, you might ask, does the airline industry have to do with currency? Well, in this case, the unit of currency we're talking about is the dreaded and unfortunate airplane accident.

The airline industry that you and I see – the one we call a carrier – is represented by a name and a logo. For example, United Airlines with its UA on the wing of every plane and its 'Fly the friendly skies of United' jingle. We see a check-in counter at the airport. We see the lounge used exclusively by business travellers. Flight attendants are the face of the airline. Bad food and free cans of soda linger in our memories. This is the airline of Mr. and Mrs. Consumer.

Looking past the airline carrier, we find the big three of airline manufacturing: Boeing, Airbus and Grumman. Beyond these are plenty of other small guys specializing in smaller planes, such as Beechcraft, Piper and Cessna. We have the fuel companies that supply the jet fuel and the airports themselves with waiting lounges, malls and McDonalds.

At the bottom of the pyramid come all the things that are invisible to us as passengers: spare parts, servicing and maintenance, the cleaning crews, the bag scanners, the baggage handlers, and even the sniffer dogs.

Now, however, suppose there is an accident. We should remind ourselves that statistically air travel is very safe, yet when there is an accident we view it with horror. And why not! In all probability, everyone on board has died. It's tragic.

For years and years, Pan-Am Airlines was a very successful American company. In many ways it represented the American Dream and the three elements that signify attainment of the American Dream: success, power, prestige. And therein lies the problem. Pan-Am's success, power and prestige made it a target for various terrorist causes and culminated in the tragic bombing of Flight 103 over Lockerbie, Scotland.

The problem with viewing the American Dream with such hostility, envy, and anger – the three curses of the weak – is that it doesn't take into account the three building blocks necessary in accomplishing the dream. These are: hard work, dedication and inventiveness.

A fatal accident is a tragic occurrence, to be sure, and the makings of news headlines far and wide. The Boeing 737 has been hijacked and blown up four times over the course of its life. And though a good 6,000 of the planes have been built since its introduction back in the late 1960's, we still get a little squeamish just thinking about it. If we really did the math, the statistics would reveal a remarkable record of one accident per 300-years of flying hours. That should make us all feel a little safer.

What, you ask, does this have to do with the Law of Thirds? It bears out three flaws of human nature:

- Fear of the unknown – we fear what we don't understand
- Power – we take solace in placing blame anywhere but on ourselves
- Blindness – we are masters at fooling ourselves.

So we conclude an accident is an extremely damaging thing to an airline carrier. Remember, people tend to recall the livery of the plane, not the make or model. A currency that turns an asset to a liability.

But an airplane accident has little impact on airport malls, fuel suppliers, or aircraft manufacturers, just because we as human beings are eager to move beyond the accident and to return to the cocoon of denial. The manufacturer might announce an industry-wide inspection of like models, or even the redesign of the model in question. No one watches too closely, because the next time we get on a plane, we want to believe all is fine and dandy. And it probably is. Still, this is in effect a form of currency.

To the bottom of the stack we go where logic tells us that an airline accident is actually good for the service and security business. Everyone gets up-in-arms for a brief bit of time, demands more attention to maintenance and repair, and what happens? More money is spent, more people are hired, and more parts are manufactured. Everyone goes home happy, including those people who were up-in-arms in the first place. Get the picture. Currency.

Viewing, as we are, an airplane accident as currency and seeing how differently each part of the airline industry is affected, we see that the same currency may have very different values depending on your perspective.

What if we take it a step further? Let's look at the currency of investments. On the whole, airline carriers are not considered the soundest of enterprises in the world's financial markets. They have three inherent investment flaws: huge debt loads, asset overload and low margins. Most financial advisors would put an 'invest at your own risk' warning on such an investment. And now that I think about it, the fleet is so heavily financed, that the one 'asset' they really own are the staff uniforms, and maybe not even those.

So what are the currencies we most often associate with airlines? At the carrier level, it's all about the face they present. It's all about the brand they create. It's all about evolving an image that really no one cares about in this day and age. Why? Because it is the cost of a ticket that is most prominent in peoples' minds. Any profits at all are generally wasted on three very obvious expenses: advertising, C-level bonuses and debt financing. Forget dividends.

Were you an investor who put $10,000 into American Airlines' stock ten years ago, you will be less than excited to know that it is now worth a little over $2,000. Suicide watch anyone? It's absolutely no wonder airline carrier investments come with a wealth warning! In total, 17 U.S. airlines have filed for bankruptcy since 2005, and who knows how many more have been victims of mergers and buyouts. A tenuous business you say? I couldn't agree more.

Back to the bottom of the stack, the guys in the servicing, spares, and repair racket. Take Rolls Royce. They're a front line supplier of aircraft turbines as well as spare parts. Look at its balance sheet. What do spares, service and maintenance generate? They generate profits. Lots of profit. What did the sale of the turbines themselves generate? A bit of excitement, but not much in the way of profits.

Some airlines are lucky to own their own maintenance companies. KLM (a nice TLA huh?), also known as the Royal Dutch Airlines, is fairly successful as carriers go. Alas, they still managed to lose money over the past three years. Their maintenance operations, however, turn a reliable profit, yielding around 10% income on a billion Euros of revenue last year. Think KLM is planning on spinning off that division any time soon? I seriously doubt it. Why? Three very profound reasons: profit, profit and more profit.

Have I left you feeling overwhelmed? Or is it making sense yet? We're still talking currency here, so let's look at the product airlines actually sell: getting you and me from point A to point B. Pretty straightforward. While that might seem like our single-issue machine from Chapter 1, it really isn't. After all, "It's not where you're going, it's how you get there."

And "It's not the destination, it's the journey." That one sounds like a life philosophy to me.

But as far as the journey via the friendly skies goes, it looks like we've got this Law of Thirds stuff mastered. That's right. I give the three ways to travel: at the sharp end, on the top deck, or at the back with the cattle – first class, business and economy. Same product, just different people, at a different price, and for different reasons.

From airlines to cinemas, from supermarkets to super conductors, from family life to home life, recognizing differing values is commonplace in what we might call a multi-layered economy. In all cases involving the issue of currency, there is more to value than just pounds, shillings and pence.

So what does this all mean? Well, for one, let's recognize that different people place different values upon different things. Now that's a fitting tribute to the Law of Thirds to be sure.

However, there's more to it. We've all seen that different things should be valued using different metrics. This is all dependent upon the currency we're dealing in: love, time, money, trust, fear, fame, power, happiness and on and on.

The balance we seek is in the careful observation of what is being spent and what is being earned. And how, you ask, do these affect the three components of freedom: life, liberty, and the pursuit of happiness?

Just remember the immortal words of Groucho Marx, "Money frees you from doing things you dislike. And since I dislike doing nearly everything, money comes in handy."

Fill your boots with the currencies that you value most and feel the freedom.

Three-Legged Stool

For a solid and stable strategy, base your idea on three equal pillars.

Need somewhere to sit? Pull up a high chair, a deck chair, a folding chair, or a lounge chair. Pull up a couch, a bench, a rocker, an ottoman, or a pew. The options are endless even if your comfort or stability might be in question.

A no-legged sitting device has its advantages. Picture yourself in sweet repose on a barrel chair, a tree trunk, or the hood of car. Just don't picture yourself sitting there for very long since comfort – or the lack thereof – is almost certainly going to become an issue.

In some cases, a one-legged device might be in order, such as a cane, a shooting stick, or a very sturdy umbrella perhaps. All can easily be carried about and propped up almost anywhere, but a one-legged device will only carry the day if you have both feet firmly planted on the ground.

Yes, you could try sitting on a Swiss exercise ball, a medicine ball, a basketball, or even a beach ball. All are inherently unstable, though all have the potential of giving you one heck of a good workout simply trying to maintain your balance. For lounging purposes, however, you might want to consider a beanbag instead.

Would a rocking chair qualify as a two-legged sitting device? I suppose it would. And the advantage in this case is a well-designed structure that always returns to a position of equilibrium no matter how aggressively you disturb it. Thus their popularity with all age groups.

The four-legged sitting device is most often called a chair, whether it's a dinner chair, a director's chair, a captain's chair, or hard-back chair. Most fit neatly under a dining table, and most can be arranged in any configuration as long at the surface in question is fairly level. Put a four-legged chair on an uneven surface or the slightest of slopes, and you'll find yourself in a precarious position to be sure.

Which brings us to the three-legged stool, a tribute to the Law of Thirds if ever there was one.

To begin with, a three-legged stool is stable on most surfaces, uneven or otherwise. The distribution of weight balanced against three equally-sized and symmetrically-placed legs is cause for remarkable stability, and our brains in their most natural state are always in search of stability.

The three-legged-stool generally is fixed with a round, flat seat which allows for maneuverability, encourages flexibility, and rewards dexterity, three very rewarding attributes for the nimble man, woman, or child.

A tripod is not a stool, but it is a device with three legs that offers the cameraman, the photographer, the surveyor, or the marksman a device that provides the very same balance between stability and flexibility that the stool does for sitting, leaning, or perching; not an unintended reference to the Law of Thirds, in case you were wondering.

How about mounting a sign to a wall, a train, bus, or trolley car? These are all cases where a three point fixation is often the method of choice, especially when time is of the essence and materials are at a premium. Two up and one down, like an inverted triangle; or one up and two down, like a pyramid formation.

Let's take a quick peek at the three-legged stool of defense. Most nations feature the Army, Navy and Air Force. And if we look inside the vaunted naval fleet of the UK we find their three invincible class carriers: Ark Royal, Illustrious and Invincible. Despite the economic problems that no one of right mind would consider anything but normal fare for the UK, nobody ever questions reducing the fleet. And why should they? Three of anything always seems a sensible and measured number, even when it comes to billion dollar vessels of destruction.

Here's a quick reminder. Whether it's military spending, politics as usual, or business at the corporate level, you will never be criticized for commissioning a three pillar strategy. The human brain is drawn to the idea of thirds like a bear is to a honey jar; it just makes sense.

Okay, and yes, there is also what some would call the three-plus-one strategy, and this is very often a ploy in the arenas of defense, politics, or business where the possibility of needing to swap out one of the stool's three legs exists. So once again, the UK's naval force helps prove the point. I give you the Vanguard Class submarines, all four of them. Why four, you ask? Because it is assumed that one will always have to be in port undergoing some sort of maintenance and repair, leaving the common man the assurance that there will always be three such submarines roaming the ocean floor in case war breaks out and some pesky dictator needs a good thrashing.

The three-plus-one is a very common strategy when it comes to clustering computer servers. Once again, we have a back-up to the three machines working overtime in the name of information technology just in case one crashes or needs to pay a visit to the shop, as we all need to from time to time.

Or how about school terms? We've mentioned already that the three school terms were based on the three 'natural' seasons. But what happens if sickness or an accident impacts a student's progress? You guessed it! It's off to summer school.

What about planning your retirement? We call this the three-legged stool of support. Why? The first pillar represents the state benefits that you are due. The second pillar signifies well-deserved employment benefits. And the third leg of support comes from your own private savings. Oh yes, and did we mention that there may also be a fourth? Yes, you guessed it. It's the ever more prevalent 'back-up plan', better known as working after retirement.

What about the three-legged stool of understanding? Clearly, this stool is held up by history, languages and mathematics. As one very astute gentleman named Robert Heinlein once said, "…if you lack any one of them you are just another ignorant peasant with dung on your boots." Now that's nicely put.

Want one more? How about the three-legged stool of creativity? First, you have imagination. Second, you have connectedness. Third, you have desire. Remove any of the three, and the passion for your craft disappears into thin air, and you are left with the art of going through the motions.

Freedom

Free thinking is the prerequisite for all other freedoms.

Freedom has many definitions, and most are directly related to the Law of Thirds. And by this time, I doubt you're surprised. Freedom can be expressed as:

- Freedom of movement
- Freedom to produce
- Freedom to consume.

Freedom was first defined in the Declaration of Independence as the pursuit of three inseparables:

- Life
- Liberty
- The Pursuit of Happiness.

Others define it by citing the three liberties:

- Natural liberty: this is the license to act without constraint, restricted only by what causes immediate harm to others
- Civil liberty: this is the right to do what may not be best for me but is the right thing to do, within the realm of a presumed absolute morality
- Essential liberty: this is what people deserve based simply on their humanity.

Freedom of thought is just as important as freedom of physical movement and freedom of consumption. Benjamin Franklin once said, "Without freedom of thought, there is no wisdom."

And we asserted right from the first pages of this book that everything around us is due to our own thoughts as well as the thoughts of others. And thus:

- We think, we conceive
- We think, we push the envelope
- We think, we challenge convention.

In fact, without our own thoughts and the thoughts of others, there would be nothing to consume – both literally and figuratively – and there would be no means for physical movement, above and beyond our own mobility. Forget bullet trains, Ferraris and Lear Jets.

I see it this way: free thinking is the prerequisite for all other freedoms. Mark Twain put it another way. He said, "It is by the fortune of God that in this country we have three benefits: freedom of speech, freedom of thought and the wisdom never to use either." There are times when Mr. Twain's point seems well taken, especially when it comes to politics.

The first amendment of the US Constitution is most often cited for its remarkable insight in granting three fundamental freedoms:

- Freedom of speech
- Freedom to the press
- Freedom to assembly.

Ironic how often these come under attack. I wonder how appealing life would be in the United States without them. Not very.

Freedom goes deep into the realm of communications. The three prerequisites most notable in this area are: communications without limitation, without censorship and without suppression.

This communication discussion can be expanded to include the freedom to adopt the view of others, to play devil's advocate and to change your mind. Once again, a clear-cut nod to the Law of Thirds.

You've heard the saying, "Put yourself in my shoes." Or, "Walk a mile in my shoes." Interestingly, this is a powerful expression of freedom. Putting yourself in someone else's shoes improves our ability to communicate, understand and empathize, which is priceless. It allows us to revisit past communications and to anticipate communications to come. We don't need hindsight and we don't need a time machine. We just need the ability to express our freedom of thought.

How does this relate to the Law of Thirds? Well, in three years you will be three years older. You will have three years' more experience. You will have three fewer years to pay off your mortgage. In my case, however, my credit card will surely have the same balance in three years if I don't change my ways.

Just as important, I think we would all agree, is the freedom to:

- Reject the ideas of others
- Pass judgment on the ideas of others
- Make assumptions about the ideas of other.

I like this one: if this guy is rich, he must be doing something right. If this guy is really rich, he must be doing everything right. Ah, the beauty of assumptions. Yes, it's our right to make them, but assumptions do have a way of making us look silly.

Freedoms, however, are not open-ended. There are three freedom no-nos. You do not have the right to harm another person. You do not have the right to defame another's character. You do not have the right to incite hatred, or use hate speech.

What is most important in this discussion is the three rules of freedom.

- Never take your freedom for granted
- Never infringe upon the freedoms of another
- Never use your freedoms to cause harm or injury.

And always remember these inimitable words. "Freedom is not worth having if it does not include the freedom to make at least three mistakes." Gandhi

Triage

If you know you will need to function under extreme pressure, or you need other people to perform tasks under excessive stress, make sure they have simple instructions that can be carried out automaton like.

Triage actually means dividing into three groups. It's a medical term defining the act of categorizing patients according to acuity and their need for treatment.

So what are these three groups?

- Patients who are dead or about to die; in other words, those for whom treatment will not prevent the loss of life
- Patients who need immediate treatment; in other words, those who can be saved
- The walking wounded who do not require immediate attention.

The term comes from the French, and, not surprisingly, advances three simple actions: separate, sort and sift. In war time, triage led to three slightly less simple actions: determining the order and priority of emergency treatment, the order and priority of emergency transport, or the transport destination for the patient.

Triage is about taking action, and it's not just for medical experts. It's for anyone who might face a situation where his or her presence of mind might make the difference between life and death.

There are three primary triage systems:

- Simple triage sorts patients into those who need critical attention and immediate transport to the hospital and those with less serious injuries
- Simple triage and rapid treatment is a simple triage system that can be performed by lightly-trained lay and emergency personnel in emergencies
- Advanced triage is where doctors may actually decide that some seriously injured people should not receive advanced care because they are unlikely to survive.

For you and I, the need for triage at any level will probably never happen, but what if it does? What if you're at the scene of an accident or caught in a devastating earthquake or tsunami? Ask yourself how you would react in an emergency situation surrounding a car accident, a natural disaster such as a hurricane, or a person choking on a bit of food in a restaurant. Would you act, freeze, or hesitate?

Let's say you are a first responder at such a tragedy. Then what? There are three TLAs to remember. The first is PAM, which stands for the Patient Assist Method. The first step in PAM, which is also the second TLA, is the establishment of a Casualty Collection Point or CCP. This is the place where you'll urge anyone requiring assistance to gather. And the third acronym is CPR, which stands for CardioPulmonary Resuscitation, an emergency procedure for people in cardiac arrest or, in some circumstances, respiratory arrest.

CPR is best remembered by three easy steps:

- Call: after you've checked and found a victim unresponsive, call 911(or other emergency number)
- Blow: if the victim isn't breathing normally, pinch nose, cover their mouth with yours and blow until you see the chest rise
- Pump: if the victim is still not breathing normally, coughing or moving, begin chest compressions.

Let your brain act in its most natural fashion and all your training will come back to you.

Remember: think in thirds.

Placebo Effect

Something that you interpret as doing very little can mean a lot to someone else.

Let's say right off the bat that our discussion surrounding placebos and the placebo effect coincides with remarkable consistency to the Law of Thirds. The very definition subscribes to the theory:

A placebo is an inactive, fake, or dummy medication or treatment designed to resemble a drug or treatment and is given in the same way as the real thing.

Did you see it? The three qualities of a placebo: inactive, fake, or dummy. Any improvement in health that is measured, observed, or felt after the placebo is given is called the placebo effect. There it is again. The three discernable elements of the placebo effect: measured, observed, or felt.

What about the three groups of every drug trial? They look like this:

1. Those patients taking no drug
2. Those patients taking a placebo drug
3. Those patients taking the actual drug.

The placebo effect is, in essence, a celebration of a very important third way of acting or taking action. This is a very logical progression that we often ignore. In effect, we should always remember that when we are to decide when to do something, or when not to do something, there is always a third placebo option of appearing to do something. This is not a figment of our imaginations. This is, in fact, a growing behavioral trait in our society. As in, if I appear to be doing something, I may actually get away with doing nothing.

At first glance, this behavioral trait seems deceitful. For instance, if my boss comes over to my desk, should I switch to a spreadsheet so I appear to do something? Well, not quite. One, who do I think I'm fooling? And two, isn't it just easier to actually be doing something?

Or, maybe there's a more constructive way of looking at it. If my boss thinks I'm working on an Excel spreadsheet, then perhaps the placebo actually did its job. He goes away thinking he's inspired and motivated me, and I feel good knowing I've put a bit of spring in my boss' step. Hail the placebo!

A placebo doesn't have to be a pill or a drug. Keep in mind the three physiological placebos: thoughts, inferences and expectations. Oh, how powerful these can be in today's world.

Here is this striking example of what we might call an anti-placebo, as it were. Women who believe they're prone to heart disease are nearly four times as likely to die from it as women with similar risk factors who don't hold such fatalistic views.

It has been proven over and over again that children who go to school armed with their parents' expectation of good performance will do far better than a student of similar intellect who comes to school with no expectations.

If a businessman is having a cocktail after work with his colleagues and makes inference to an insider trading tip he's got about a penny stock that's about to take off, that inference will drive someone from his group to jump up the next morning, go online, and invest who knows how much in the stock.

Here's one we've all run into. We check into a hotel and are told our room isn't quite ready. So sorry, the guest before you just left. What if we give you an upgrade? The word upgrade might very well be the most potent placebo going. Your upgraded hotel room turns out to be exactly the same room that you reserved, but the bed feels so much more comfortable, because, after all, it's an upgrade.

Go to the supermarket; if it's one you often shop at, you could well be in possession of a loyalty card. The placebo of having a few points added to your balance at the checkout diverts attention away from how much you're spending to how many points you are accumulating. Of course to the supermarket, offering a 1% credit is well worth the loyalty of its shoppers. And besides, deep down, we all know they simply add that 1% back into the prices their loyal customers are paying. What a con!

The car industry is famous for its placebo effect. You bring your new car in with some mechanical ailment and the logical step would be to replace the car with no questions asked. Not on your life. Most likely the faulty part will be repaired, which doesn't help if the part is faulty, or the faulty part is replaced, which isn't likely to help if the part hasn't been redesigned. The placebo effect is a little trick the dealer calls a free valet service to and from work or a free courtesy car. You suddenly feel special, valued and exclusive. No, that's just the placebo getting you to settle down and accept whatever diagnosis your mechanic happens to make.

Placebos in almost all circumstances represent a grain of hope. Oh, what we won't do for a grain of hope. That's all we really want out of life. Just a ray of sunshine to make us think everything is going to be okay.

You've heard of the three elements of hope. That's what the placebo effect is all about: creating hope. So what are these three elements?

1. The first element of hope is the affirmation that the future is positive and good
2. The second element of hope is the confidence that change will make a difference
3. The third element of hope is that my actions can make a difference.

As the prisoner in the Shawshank Redemption says to his fellow inmate, "Hope is the best of all things." And so it is. And that's why placebos work.

Then there is what I call the reverse placebo. This is the ubiquitous effort on the part of buyers and sellers alike in promoting the idea of getting something out of nothing. The best and most obvious examples are the now-omnipresent TV infomercials. It's almost impossible to avoid them, but it's also amazing how prolific they have become. Why? They must work. Buy the new and improved Thigh-Buster for $9.99 with a money back guarantee if it doesn't trim your thighs within two weeks. There are three irresistible placebos at work here:

1. First, the price, which is irresistibly low, backed by the tiny print alerting you to a $6.99 delivery charge, which the buyer conveniently ignores
2. Second, the new and improved promise, which convinces us that this is the model that has been made specifically for us (the old model just wasn't quite up to it)
3. And third, the guarantee; no matter how unrealistic their promise, we want to believe that trimming our thighs in two weeks actually is possible. And hopefully we won't have to work to see the results.

We saw in the currency section how the value of an engine turbine holds little profit for the manufacturer, yet it's the most important part of an airplane. And we saw how the service charges keep the manufacturer in business, yet they end up becoming a single line item on the company's financial statement. The placebo in this case is particularly subtle and pays tribute in kind to the Law of Thirds. How? Because it is unseen, unappreciated and beyond important.

Okay, so now let's talk about the self-placebo. What are the three basics of the self-placebo? One, it's a thought, idea, or consideration that we impose upon ourselves. Two, we don't recognize it as a placebo. Three, it satisfies an urge without providing concrete results. Here's a good example for you. What's the upside of being rich? Most people would say, "I would want for nothing." Translated, anything they wanted, they could buy. It's the thought that qualifies as the placebo. Whether it's true or not that they could buy anything they wanted, it's a nice idea that satisfies the question.

Spontaneous buying is another example of a self-placebo. There is a sense of power and satisfaction – though short-lived at best – in walking into a shop or kiosk and buying something at random, whether it's a magazine, newspaper, or a candy bar. The spontaneity of the action leaves you with a momentary 'rich' feeling. This is the placebo in action!

What about an inspirational magazine? What will it be? Jet Pilot Weekly, Mega Yacht Monthly, Country House Today? They give you all the sense of being there, with glossy images and enveloping prose, but without the hassle of submitting flight plans, dealing with the marina staff, or listening to nail guns and circular saws while you try and sip your mint julep.

The same psychology that makes a dummy medication so profound is also behind the spontaneous purchase, whether it's a $100,000 Porsche or a $1 Butterfinger candy bar. There are three keys that are ever consistent in this wicked little process:

1. The first key is the ease with which you make the purchase
2. The second key is the sense of satisfaction that comes with acting flippant and self-absorbed
3. The third key is the momentary feeling of power that comes when you toss aside the candy wrapper or abandon the magazine on the bus without a thought.

The placebo is personal. Placebos work because you and I want them to work. And they work because the Law of Thirds sees an advantage in allowing the brain to process even something that is merely measured, observed, or felt. It can still be real, even if it's not.

Use the placebo yourself, use them on your customers, use them on your colleagues; the value will always exceed the cost.

Color

When faced with what seems like an infinite list of things to process or large amounts of data, it can almost certainly be represented by using three fields.

Let's look, for example, at how the eye works when it sees green grass. The eyes of mammals like you and I are composed of two types of receptors: rod receptors and cone receptors. Rod receptors are primarily responsible for greater night vision and movement tracking, while cone receptors allow for color processing and greater daytime vision. You won't be shocked to find that there are three types of cones:

- Short-wavelength sensitive cones, which scientists call the S-cone
- Middle-wavelength sensitive cones, which they call the M-cone
- Long-wavelength sensitive cones, which they call the L-cone.

The three receptor cones can also be noted as the green cone, the red cone and the blue cone. Yes, I'm simplifying, but you get the picture. So when the eye falls upon a field of green grass, the green cone will send the brain the largest, most dynamic signal, while the red and blue cones take a backseat. This allows the eye to perceive millions of different shades, using just three different cells.

The receptor cones are also blessed with three ranges of spectral sensitivity. Blue sensitivity, for example, gives us the ability to see in starlight. Red sensitivity allows us to perceive heat.

In contrast to the eye, the human ear has many thousands of nerves along the length of the cochlea and each nerve responds to a particular pitch. In theory, there exists just one cell for each single note. However, research in this area has essentially debunked this archaic notion, and current thinking now suggests that three distinct ear cells are responsible for determining the exact pitch of a note: the inner ear cells, the outer ear cells and the supporting ear cells.

This pitch sharpening mechanism is part of the brain's natural function and goes a long way in explaining why some very lucky souls are blessed with perfect pitch. Yes, I know this has nothing to do with color, but I couldn't resist adding to our list of relevant thirds, and this seemed the perfect place.

So, digressing no more, let's go back to our study of color and the way the Law of Thirds influences sight. May I introduce the three visual 'opics': photopic, mesopic and scotopic. These very lofty scientific terms refer to the three ranges of our vision acuity, each depending on how much light the eye is exposed to at any given time. Yes, this is far too complicated for our discussions, but it is revealing when it comes to the consistency of thirds even in the human anatomy.

Night vision describes our ability to see in a dark environment; pretty obvious. Less obvious is that night vision is made possible by a combination of three relevant approaches: sufficient spectral range, sufficient intensity range and a sufficient heat source. We would describe the color generated by a heat source in the dark as white or some shade of white, since night vision relegates color to shades of black and white essentially.

Okay, enough about color. What does this all mean to you and me and the man on the street? And how can we apply it to our lives?

When faced with what seems like an infinite list of things to process or an excruciatingly large amount of data to sort out, it can almost certainly be represented in an effective way using three attributes.

We might have a million things to do, but they can all be listed under the three levels of the here and now: urgency, value and importance. Our health is of intrinsic importance – we would all agree with that – and yet it is only on the rare occasion when it is urgent. What's more, we normally associate it with a cost rather than a value. A task might be urgent and have tangible and near-term value, and yet it may be of little importance to strategic direction.

How about a more literal example? If you go to hospital, you will most certainly be asked to identify yourself. Name, date of birth and street address; and yes, perhaps a social security number if you live in the States or a national insurance number if you live in Britain. This is then all fed into a vast database of medical records and they see if it all matches up. Remarkable that even with many millions of records these three important pieces of information are enough to reference pretty much everyone and to do so uniquely and efficiently.

Color and the Law of Thirds are irrevocably linked. Want a reminder? Jump in your car, pull up to a stoplight and watch how the natural process of your brain dissects the three commands of the stoplight: red, stop; yellow, slow down; green, go.

And go we shall onto our next section dedicated to winners.

Winners

If your strategy involves more than three ways, means or ends, eliminate the fourth, drop the fifth, and forget the sixth. Only the best three will ever be remembered.

How do we define a winner according to the Law of Thirds? There are, if you look closely, three definable traits:

1. A winner is that person who is successful based upon praiseworthy ability and hard work
2. A winner is that person or team who is determined to be the victor, especially in games and sports
3. A winner is that person who wins the admiration and respect of others.

A winner is also a thing. You know, as in, that was a definite winner. That could be a last second goal in a soccer or hockey match. That could be a blockbuster of a movie, a hit song, or the perfect prom dress. Still, a definite winner is also the product of three marked qualities:

1. A winner is a thing that brings people to their feet
2. A winner is a thing that leaves people satisfied
3. A winner is a thing that brings you back for more.

I will say this. Most of us are rather generous in our willingness to crown people or things as winners. Take the Olympic Games for instance and the winners' podium so very nicely highlighted on the previous page. The Olympics is admirable in its praise for its three podium places: first, second and third. Or, by color: gold, silver and bronze. This tradition of honoring three contestants is not only acceptable in the minds of most aficionados of these time-honored games, but it is also highly touted as demonstrating civility and class.

And quite naturally, a resounding three cheers most commonly hails the ascension of our three winners to the podium. Hip, hip, hooray. Though, I must confess, there are those in this business of cheerleading that claim a difference between a cheer and a chant. A cheer, they say, is longer and said, shouted, or sung only once. A chant, they claim, is abbreviated and bellow, barked, or bawled three times. Maybe that's why the brain is more engaged when chanting as opposed to cheering. Think about it.

In the world of track and field as well as swimming, races are traditionally kicked off with an idiom best described as 'On your marks, get set, go'. This is standard starting line jargon for everything from Easter egg hunts and drag racing to game shows and thrill seeking. This archaic, yet always current three line idiom does three things: it gets the blood churning; it instills a sense of urgency; it brings the crowd to the edge of their seats.

We talked earlier in the book about a court of law and the three elements of the less-than-perfect judicial service. As you recall, the players of note were the judge, plaintiff and defense. But when a witness approaches the stand, puts their hand on the bible, and the oath is sworn, it is a time-worthy, ascending triptych that sets the tone, as in, "Do you swear to tell the truth, the whole truth, and nothing but the truth?" This, I suppose, is meant to instill a sense of calm and thoroughness to the proceedings, quite opposite to the adrenaline inducing, "Ready, set, go." Yet, when it comes to winners in a court of law, there is hardly anything more ambiguous than "The truth, the whole truth, and nothing but the truth."

You've heard people say, "On three. One, two, three. Go!" Why three? Because "On four. One, two, three, four. Go!" sounds like an eternity. "On two. One, two. Go!" is just too quick. The natural process of the brain loves the continuity, the sense of pace, and the symmetry of "On three. One, two, three!" even if we reverse the order and proclaim, "Three. Two. One. Go!" The meaning is the same. So is the timing, the anticipation and the readiness. Yes, a suitable tribute once again to the power of thirds.

Oh, yes, lest we forget some of the old standbys:

1. Ready, set, go!
2. Ready, aim, fire!
3. Lights, camera, action!

These are all precursors to the celebration of someone winning at something, though the end result of "ready, aim, fire" might not fit that description.

Let's also emphasize that the size of the field, the number of participants, or the nature of the events do not influence the balance of our podium: gold, silver, bronze, or first, second, or third. Not at all.

A look, for example, at the world-renowned Tour de France bicycle race will paint this picture in glowing terms. Upwards of 200 riders enter this prestigious event every year, and while they do give out awards for the Best New Rider or the King of the Mountain, what really matters are the three riders who finish the 2,000 mile or so ride in first, second and third place. No one cares about the guy in fourth.

The Boston Marathon features 20,000 runners. Does this extraordinary participation make any difference to the Law of Thirds and the natural thought process of our brains? Not in the least. Awards are given out to just three of those 20,000. The guys or girls who cross the line one, two and three.

The Kentucky Derby might field 20 or more horses for its famous race and yet, the bettor is only rewarded for win, place, and show finishes.

We love our thirds. It's not that we necessarily view every other horse, runner or biker in the race as losers. Not at all. We all admire the three qualities of competition:

1. Participation
2. Hard work
3. Sacrifice.

But the memory only serves one master, and that is the Law of Thirds. Therefore, fame, admiration and longevity are decorated with the three colors of glory: gold, silver and bronze.

What are the three discernable traits that separate the winner from the loser? Well, check this out.

Losers:

1. Don't define their goals
2. Don't take the time to explore their goals or dreams
3. Don't even really consider their goals or dreams believable, much less achievable.

Winners, on the other hand:

1. Are always able to say where they're going
2. Are always able to say what they plan to do along the way
3. Are always able to say what they hope to find when they get there.

Winners also have a clear understanding of the Law of Thirds. They know when they've taken on too much, they know when they're not taking on enough and they know when they've achieved a suitable balance. The magic number, of course, is always three.

Traffic Lights

Give the gray area equal rank to the black and the white.

You know the drill. Red, yellow (amber), green. That's right, these are the three colors of the traffic light, known in almost all parts of the world as the universal symbol of stop, slow down, go.

The question is, do we really know what the colors mean and where this great tribute to the Law of Thirds comes from? If you have a driving theory test coming up in the next two weeks, then maybe you do. For the rest of us, the colors are internalized into our brains, compliments to our natural thought process.

Let's put it this way. The traffic light wasn't invented overnight and didn't just drop from the sky the day after Henry Ford came out with his Model-T. Long before roads needed traffic lights, railways were using a system of signals to control train traffic. In the early days of railways, way back in the early 1840s, trains traveled back and forth on the same, single track. This was tricky. Timing was everything. The signals back then consisted of three insanely simple parts: a pole, a ball and a kite. When the kite was raised to the top of the pole, it was a sign of danger; train approaching, wait or be crushed. When the ball was raised to the top of the pole, it signaled all clear. Time to rock 'n' roll.

Then things evolved. In 1841, the first semaphore – the term used for a visual form of signaling – was installed at London station. This device consisted of a signal arm that moved up and down across the track. It was designed with three insanely simple positions. The horizontal position told the engineer to stop. The 45-degree position across the track urged the engine driver to proceed with caution. The vertical position told the driver the track was all clear.

Even back then, the signals were painted red because it was easy to identify, even from a distance, and the color red, as it does with almost every creature, caught the driver's attention.

At night, an oil lamp was added on top of these semaphore poles with different colored glass. Even back then, a red light meant stop. However, they hadn't yet got very creative and used a white light to signal the all clear and to tell the driver to proceed with caution. The white light proved disastrous. Some took it to mean all clear, others saw it as a warning, and the result was one accident after another. Plus, white lights were being used for streetlights and porch lights and flashlights, so you can imagine the confusion.

The on-going calamities led to a modified system with the customary red light signaling stop, and a yellow light urging the driver to proceed with caution. Then a bell was added to warn the driver that the lights were about to change. The green light was not far behind. Talk about sophistication.

Since this highly evolved system was working so well with the railroads, civic officials in London decided to try it out in the city's congested streets. Thus, even before the advent of motorcars, traffic lights were introduced in 1868 in London to control the flow of the city's three major forms of congestion: horse buggies, wagons and pedestrians. Did I mention sophistication?

Enter the automobile and real confusion; cars driving here and there with no sense of order and no sense of what having the right of way might mean. It was a police officer named William Potts, a native of Detroit, Michigan, who decided to do something about the problem. And what he did was adapt railroad signals for street use.

His real problem was that street traffic didn't just run one way or another. Now there were intersections, right angles and four-way traffic. A real pain, but at least we were talking in thirds.

Potts' first signal lights employed only two colors, red and green, and were run via electricity. Thus, the first traffic light was duly installed in 1920 on the corner of Woodward and Michigan Avenues in Detroit. History in the making.

Eventually, someone realized that the human brain functioned much better according to the Law of Thirds and added the yellow light in the center of the configuration, and we're still living with that today.

In a very real sense, the yellow caution light positioned between the red and green lights – go and stop – is a tribute to the idea of giving the gray area between the black and white an equal ranking. In terms of the three cognitive arenas – perception, problem solving and action – black, white and gray represent the three areas of spatial thought.

Think of it this way: most often, a project that we undertake or an activity we engage in will have a goal or target. With every goal, there is a strategy. And for every strategy, you have tactics to implement it. The goal may have black and white implications, or, in other words, specific measures of success or failure. And while it might be normal to place parameters on these measures, most often the outcome will fall somewhere in between: in the gray area.

Consider a product roll out for a manufacturing company. Even before the product is produced, the company tests the market, conducts focus groups and gauges consumer acceptance. The results of these kinds of exploratory measures place the product, hypothetically, at the decision-making crossroads staring up at an industrial traffic light, as it were. If the test results have been a smashing success, clearly a green light signals full speed ahead. Poor test results, on the other hand, will likely produce a big flashing red light, and management might even go so far as to pull the product.

The gray area we're discussing here would, in this case, be represented by the amber/yellow light. This would no doubt be precipitated by mixed results and a plethora of questions. What is the product missing? Where did the company's planning go awry? How did we so completely miss our audience? And so on. The gray area is a place to pull back, sift through what's known and what's not known, and rethink strategy. You might call these the three penumbras of strategic planning.

But just like that all-important moment when you're driving down the road and the traffic light up ahead clicks from green to amber, the gray area is a place where decisions have to be made, and the best managers are those who can read the signals most clearly. Do you take the yellow light to mean hit the gas and blast ahead? We've all done that. Or do you take it to mean stop, consider your options, and then proceed according to your deliberations? This is what we call the three paths of accountability. Sounds pretty lofty to me. Still, we face the gray area or the amber light in various ways almost every day of our lives.

Here's an example from left field if ever there was one. You recall our discussion earlier on about the issue of personal identity. Well how about the Hijra (transvestite) people of the Indian Subcontinent? Their claim to fame is being recognized in places like Pakistan and Bangladesh as the third sex, a distinct gender recognized with equality to male and female. This is taking the concept of dynamic thirds to a whole new level, and maybe the rest of the world could learn something from it.

In any case, traffic lights – or the many symbolic traffic lights that flash in front of our faces everyday – are helpful tools, even worthwhile guideposts. But the debate will always center around the three ambiguities of choice:

- Are humans blessed with free will?
- Are humans subjected to determinism (the view that all current and future events are causally necessitated by past events combined with the laws of nature)?
- Are humans the product of karma?

Well, that may well be a debate worthy of another book entirely. In any case, the traffic lights will always be there: red, yellow and green. They can't be ignored. So why not put the Law of Thirds to good use. You can act, you can consider, or you can do nothing.

The Art of Effective Communication

Don't let the message overtake the meaning.

Let's introduce this section with the three keys to effective communication:

- Honesty. I know, this seems almost too obvious, but good communication really is built on mutual respect, and respect depends on, yes, honesty. If you want to get off on the right foot, try a heavy dose of honesty right from the get-go
- Tact. Didn't we just stress the importance of honesty? But winning your audience over also calls for tact. If you push the wrong button, the communication train will jump its track pretty quick and all the honesty in the world won't get it back on
- Wisdom. Yes, wisdom. Why? Because wisdom is the key to being tactful, of course. Unfortunately, sometimes the only path to wisdom is experience, so you may have to trip and fall every once and a while.

The real problem with effective communication and mastering the art of getting your message across is data overload. Think of the daily bombardment of images and information we all face. How are we supposed to cope with such an onslaught? How are we supposed to compete with it? How can we distinguish one voice from the next, one sound bite from another? How many different camera angles can we really handle of the TV news anchor before dizziness and disillusionment set in?

You've heard this one before (or maybe you haven't) but even if you haven't, your brain knows best. The question is this: how many typefaces are too many for one project, one billboard, one business card, one menu, one of anything written on a computer, a word processor, or a handheld device of any kind? How do you know where to draw the line? The answer: a generally accepted practice for anyone trying to communicate effectively, that is, anyone not trying to drive his or her reader completely up a wall, is to limit the number to three different typefaces. Are you surprised? Probably not after all the evidence we've presented in support of the Law of Thirds, which is not to say that you can't use more than three, but be prepared to offend the natural thought process of your already hardworking brain if you do.

If you'd like to confuse your reader, use a different typeface for every headline, every highlight and every quote. That should increase the loyalty of your audience; or send them off the deep end or to another source of information. It's simple really: more than three typefaces cause three obvious cerebral reactions: it overwhelms the brain, it distracts the thought process and it confuses the message.

Using exactly three typefaces, on the other hand, produces three predictable cerebral reactions: the design of the page, card, or memo becomes part of the meaning itself; the brain views the message as one organized thought; and the meaning behind the message is remembered in conjunction with the headline.

Too Many *Typefaces* overtake *the* message

What a mess!

God gave us three primary props for supporting our verbal communication forays; a right hand, a left hand and a very expressive face.

Observe the politician in action; there's no better example, though in the case of the really effective politician, the hands and face can obscure almost any message.

Want to overload the brain? Try 'jazz hands'. It's pretty much guaranteed that whoever you're communicating with is sure to have no bandwidth left for whatever other message you might be attempting to convey. Whereas the international message of love in sign language uses exactly three fingers to represent the message: I-L-Y, which, of course, translates very nicely to I love you. In any case, the message is the meaning. No words need to be offered to back this one up. Try it on someone tonight and see how far it gets you!

We've heard of the old proverb: "Too many cooks spoil the broth." One new rule of thumb making its way through the design world is this: "Too many elements spoil the logo." In fact, the current trend in world design relies once again on the three basics of quality design: simplicity, minimalism, and sophistication. Not surprisingly, it was the great Leonardo da Vinci himself who put it thus: "Simplicity is the ultimate sophistication." Well said, Mr. Da Vinci.

Great literature in general is also a product of the Law of Thirds. Take for example the use of three concurrent phrases as an unmistakable vehicle for creating tension. "A night filled with evil eyes, cold winds, and whispers creeping through the trees." How evocative is that; your senses are touched on so many levels.

And for descriptions, there is nothing more effective. "The sea was a symphony of kinetic turmoil, thunderous roaring, and scents as sweet as perfume." See what I mean. If the writer dared to use four such descriptive passages and said, "The horses thundering across the prairie raised a wall of thick dust, filled the air with wild cries, scared a herd of grazing cattle, and plunged into a dark canyon," the natural process of the mind loses track of the author's intent and might even forget that he or she was talking about horses in the first place.

Lovely, luscious and leggy, paints a picture of a woman in an old-time pulp fiction novel. Sour, smug and cynical describes an over-the-hill theater actor. And in three well-crafted words, the portrait takes shape.

Speaking of books, let's talk about the Law of Thirds and its profound influence on the art and craft of writing. The rule of three is a basic principle used by all great – and even not-so-great – writers. The principle suggests that words and phrases that come in threes are inherently funnier, more satisfying, or more effective than another number. It makes sense because the natural function of any reader's brain to digest, consume and process information, descriptions and messages is far more effective in thirds: in fact, I'm proud to say that last sentence contained two such examples.

Even the most effective slogans are written according to the Law of Thirds. How about "Go, fight, win!" Or, "Yes we can!" Or, "Hip, hip, hooray!"

But these phrases are all very self-serving. They sound great, our mind sucks them in and loves how they work. But do they actually mean anything? Has the meaning we are trying to convey been overtaken by the message itself? In the end, does it really matter? Because, in the end, our brains will discard what it doesn't need, hold on to the important stuff, and give meaning to even the most nonsensical of phrases. My favorite is: "Make my day!"

Let's play with three adjectives. Warm, eager and full. Totally unrelated and hardly interchangeable. And yet, according to the three articles of literary license – these being the distortion of fact, the alteration of the conventions of grammar or language, or the rewording of pre-existing text – you will see how things don't necessarily have to relate or be interchangeable for them to work in counterposing ways. Try dissecting these three sentences, and you'll see what I mean:

- Captain William Foster unmoored his schooner and, with a full belly, a warm wind, and an eager mind, set off to his destiny
- Captain William Foster unmoored his schooner and, with a warm belly, an eager wind, and a full mind, set off to his destiny
- Captain William Foster unmoored his schooner and, with an eager belly, a full wind, and a warm mind, set off to his destiny.

These all sound great, don't they? Messages meant for a Booker Prize winning novel; well, perhaps not. In truth, this is a case of using the Law of Thirds like tomato sauce on a bad steak, and, as steaks go, a fairly rancid one at that.

And talking of steak, would you expect a restaurant menu to describe a dish with three verbs? "A dazzling, delectable, irresistible prime rib." "A savory, succulent, smoky strip steak." Wow! Talk about the message overtaking the meaning; kind of like the cooking overwhelming the ingredients.

I always say, by all means feel free to use condiments or sauces, but always taste what you're serving up without it. Why? Because there will always be those people who will be able to see straight through you, and you'll get knocked off that three-legged stool fairly quickly if you're not careful.

Don't overdo it. Know when enough is enough. And when in doubt, trust in the Law of Thirds.

Picture Art

Use the power of thirds to direct people exactly where you want them to look. Move to where you know they will go.

Picture art is a classic way of studying the Law of Thirds from a vision point of view. Picture art generally refers to three classic art forms: paintings (without regard to the media), photographs and illustrations. In all three cases, the resulting image contains three essential points of view: a background, a subject and a foreground.

Check out the illustration, perhaps it's our old friend Captain Foster heading off into the sunset?

In the foreground, the eye is drawn to the woman standing on the dock, and more specifically to the top of her head. Next, the eyes move in perfect harmony to the boat motoring away from the viewer. Finally, the eye seeks the boat's destination along the horizon in the background. Very pleasing indeed.

This leads us in the most natural fashion to the three rules of composition. They are:

- Rule of Thirds: this is based on the fact that the human eye is naturally drawn to a point about two-thirds up a page. A good photographer, painter, or illustrator breaks his or her work into nine equal squares or rectangles, and then makes sure that the main subjects are located around one of the intersection points rather than in the center of the image. I'll buy that
- Golden section rule: this is all about the fact that certain points in a picture's composition automatically attract the viewer's attention. It also refers to the fact that many natural or man-made objects and scenes with certain proportions (whether by chance or by design) automatically please us. Common sense
- Diagonal rule: in this case, one side of the picture is divided into two, and then each half is divided into three parts. The adjacent side is divided so that the lines connecting the resulting points form a diagonal frame. Thus, the important elements of the picture should be placed along these diagonals. Logical.

Isn't it interesting to note that an SLR camera will focus on the center of the shot, but, as we're now finding out, this is normally not where the eye will be drawn when looking at the final photograph?

On the other hand, a good number of today's more modern cameras have a viewfinder grid to allow you to place the important elements of a photo – this could be a person's face or a beautiful sunset – exactly where the eye will go when the viewer is scrutinizing the final product. Makes sense, of course. The grids, we should note here, are all built upon the Law of Thirds. Three grids across, three down and three diagonal; a perfect match for the brain's natural functions.

But I don't want to confine our thinking to photo art alone. The best painters, the best designers, even the best sculptures honor the human eye's natural tendency toward the three rules of visual acuity: clarity, placement and positioning.

Picture yourself walking into an empty auditorium. You have your choice of seats. Any seat at all. Inevitably, you will be drawn by the same rules that dictate a well-crafted painting, illustration, or photo, one that draws your eye to crucial elements placed according to the three rules described above. You will naturally choose a seat with a vantage point that is neither too close nor too far away, but also one neither too low nor too high. But, don't be surprised if sitting in the exact middle isn't also a little uncomfortable. Perfect isn't always the answer, because the brain always needs something to work on.

This also works in the two-dimension world as well. An example, you say? How about choosing a urinal in a public bathroom? Yes, position counts every time.

But how can this power be harnessed? After all, we don't always get to choose exactly where our shop or store is located on a particular street. We don't always get to dictate where our product appears on a supermarket shelf. No, but we can make sure that the picture art we use to advertise our shop or product is created with the natural functions of the brain in mind.

Bullet points are not picture art per se, but more and more in our sound bite world we see the use of bullet points as a technique for drawing the eye. Like picture art, bullet points are designed to satisfy the three laws of grabbing someone's attention: catch the eye, draw the eye, focus the eye. But what bullet points can't do that picture art can is hold the eye.

There is another problem with bullet points and highlighting within written text and that should be addressed here, at least in short. Unlike picture art, the writer has little control on where these things will land in the text or on the page. That's the computer's job, and, unless you're willing to mess with the acceptable formatting process, you're a slave to the computer.

Can a letter be viewed as picture art? I suppose it depends on how badly you want your letter to influence the recipient. What about a postcard? Or even an email?

Keep in mind the three rules of visual communication

- Does it get your message across?.
- Does it move the viewer to take action?
- Does it leave a lasting impression?

Picture art is like someone calling your name. If it's done right, you turn around and take notice. Three things happen: you're captivated, you're moved and you want to respond.

It's like printing your name on the front of an envelope. If it's handwritten, it will always get your attention far more than if it's typed. If it's positioned correctly, just like the most important elements in a painting, your eye goes right to it. Then you take a moment to look at the return address, the postmark, even the envelope. Then you open. Voila! Time to read. Now there seems to be a trend towards adding a line in bold, capitalized lettering beneath the recipient's name on modern business letters. A subject line, just like on an email. Of course, this is to emphasize what the sender wants from the communication even before you open the letter or the email.

Now whether this is an appropriate way to compose a letter is not for me to say, but there is no end of people who consider using a recipient's favorite proper noun as a way of putting them in a positive frame of mind before you come right out and ask for whatever it is you need to ask them for. I think we call this buttering them up, but it's somewhat like using picture art to frame a controversy or disaster. Is this making any sense?

Let me clarify. This is very important point with regard to communication on any level, including that of picture art. You've heard of the three steps of a masterful presentation, I'm sure. Well here they are:

1. Open by telling your audience what you will tell them
2. Tell your audience what you intend to tell them
3. Then tell your audience what you just told them.

This is the Law of Thirds at work. It's not manipulation. It's using the natural thought process of the brain to its full advantage, even when your communication vehicle is photography, painting, or illustration.

Nothing in the world wrong with that!

Three Point Turn

If the task at hand seems beyond your natural abilities, split the task up into three parts.

Sure, a London taxi can turn on a sixpence; you've heard the saying perhaps. Well, to be fair, that's just a wee bit of an exaggeration. In truth, the turning radius of a London taxi is 25 feet, assuming the driver is in full possession of his or her faculties.

But what if you find yourself on a narrower street or in a bigger car and your goal is a 180 degree turn in a narrower street? Behold the three point turn. From London to Bangkok, from Sydney to L.A., the three point turn is a universal part of driving exams worldwide. Your parents probably taught you, and you probably taught your kids.

The three point turn amounts to three distinct movements, two forward and one in reverse, just not in that order. Picture a short 90 degree turn of the car to the left, followed by a reverse turn of approximately the same angle, and straight ahead you go. Oh, yes, it's always a good idea to check your mirrors before making this maneuver, all three of them, rear and two sides.

At the heart of the three point turn is a three word idiom invaluable in situations far more complex than driving a taxi. You're heard it. You've preached it to your employees, your kids, and even to yourself. Leave yourself room to maneuver. It sounds like a politician's line, doesn't it? But the truth is, the last thing most of us want to do is to put ourselves into a corner with no options.

A good way to facilitate this idea of giving yourself room to maneuver is to look at a task, in particular one that seems beyond your natural abilities and split it up into three parts, three steps, three phases, or three whatever. Small steps often make for a giant leap. That said, the nature of such tasks, and an appropriate means of separating them into three manageable steps, might require some out of the box thinking.

The definition of a three point turn also has a philosophic bent to it as well. It references three commonly applied diversions: the slippery dodge, the last minute excuse and blatant disregard. I am not particularly good at any of these, mainly because I've been cursed with the three traits of a bad liar: a guilty conscience, a lack of practice and an overactive moral compass. Well, I guess there are worse things.

Avoiding the need for a three point turn is also a point worth considering. It goes to the question: how did you get yourself into such a mess in the first place, or the three sure ways into a bad situation. Was it bad directions, a wrong turn, or a lack of planning?

A wise man once said failing to plan equals planning to fail. That's pretty profound stuff, but it's even more remarkable how often we stumble into a situation without any clear picture of what we want or where we're going. Aristotle, an even wiser man, once told his followers: "An unplanned life isn't worth living." That might be a bit extreme, but his point is well taken nonetheless.

And since this section has been so nicely planned out, I say we follow with a brief discussion about milestones, which, of course, make such things as planning so much easier for you. What is a milestone? Not surprisingly, there are three important aspects to every milestone.

1. A specific date that indicates the completion of something
2. An event in the future that you hope to reach
3. The end of a phase or a task.

I like to put it this way. A milestone is that point in time when there is no overlapping work to cloud an important point in any endeavor. A milestone is that very natural point at which you may disengage the gear and change direction.

An easy example of milestones in action is the construction of a house. An example within our example is the foundation. Once that's been poured or laid, a basic milestone has been reached. When the walls are up and the roof is on, you've reached a second milestone. When the plumbing and electrics have been run, you've reached another. You get the idea.

A milestone is an opportunity. It affords us the chance to change tacks if we choose to. If you're set a goal to lose 30 pounds, you may set two milestones, one at ten pounds and again at 20 pounds. Each milestone allows you to celebrate an achieved goal. It also allows you, in this case, to say, hey, I'm good with losing 20 pounds. I think I'll call it good and not worry about that extra ten.

Giving yourself a milestone to shoot for requires an understanding of the three organizational necessities: plan, execute and review. You plan the steps necessary to reach your milestone; you execute those steps; you review at the end of those steps to see whether or not your milestone has been achieved. Simple, perhaps, but not necessarily easy!

In our construction example, when the house is closed in, the walls are up, and the roof is sealed, the builder may take this time to re-evaluate his or her budget. The owner may want his or her architect to make some interior changes.

In the three point turn, we also have milestones. The end of the first forward maneuver is one milestone; a point where you can keep going or change track. The end of the reverse maneuver is a second milestone; are you now ready to press forward again or do you need to reassess your position? And so on.

Milestones strongly suggest that you are taking action, being pro-active, and thus productive. But alas, that is not always the case, and leads us to discuss the three essentials of wasting time and money. You've heard of them, and you've surely practiced them. We all have. They are: procrastination, distraction and disorganization.

Don't be surprised if these lead you to a few situations where the only answer is a good, old-fashioned three point turn.

Dining

Don't get suckered into the use of thirds for comfort reasons; Be judicious and know when the law is meant to be bent.

Does the subject of dining strike you as an unusual stop for our discussion on the Law of Thirds? Nothing could be further from the truth. Let's begin with the three basic utensils found on most American or European tables: knife, fork and spoon. Yes, things get confusing when you start adding a salad fork or a dessert spoon, but it still comes back to the basics.

And speaking of basics, look no further than the three meals of the day. This is pretty easy: breakfast, lunch and dinner. But what about any worries you might have about the three linchpins of dieting: calories, food groups and nutrition? Fear not. These dietary worries can apparently be eliminated by following one of the truly great motivational tributes ever spoken in favor of the Law of Thirds:

- Eat breakfast like a king
- Eat lunch like a prince
- Eat supper like a pauper.

I love a good motivational quote as much as the next guy, and eating three meals a day is all very comforting and all, but I am one person who can't function at all after stuffing myself with a king-sized breakfast. All I want to do, frankly, is sleep. And naturally, I pay the price of this dearth of early morning fare when supper rolls around and I find myself as hungry as a bear. What's a man to do?

The answer can pretty much be summed up in, yes, three oft-spoken words: "I need food." The problem is that rarely do these cravings come in convenient, well thought applications of three: an apple, a perfectly proportioned chicken breast and a bowl of vegetable soup. No such luck indeed. It is much more likely that the craving will include a burger, a bowl of rice, gherkin, Swiss cheese, French fries, an apple turnover, a bowl of mint chocolate chip ice cream and something completely decadent to drink, like a splash of single malt Scotch or a large Coke. So much for food groups, calorie counting and good, sound nutrition.

There is an upside. My craving very often leads me to the local hamburger joint for a cheeseburger, fries, and a soda, (three all-America classics), and that tends to suffice just fine, thank you very much. Super-sized, of course.

We might also hazard a guess as to why a third of the modern world is overweight; the answer almost certainly lies with our obsession for what has come to be known as three square meals a day. The operative word is square of course, and this has become a hazardous adjective when it comes to the western view of eating. Square most often means plentiful, copious, or overflowing, none of which is optimal when it comes to eating well.

This westernized view is further distorted by a bombardment of nutritional reminders suggesting that each and every meal should incorporate elements from the now famous three main food groups. We all know them by heart, even if we occasionally ignore them: fats, carbohydrates and protein. We know we need some of all three of these; we don't necessarily like paying close attention to how much of each or in what proportions when served side by side. What fun is that!

Okay, but how about this oft-mentioned nutritional triumvirate: vitamins, minerals and fiber. The body needs them, not to burn as it were, but to function properly. Vitamins, minerals and fiber are a must for everything from healthy eyes, skin and hair to strong and properly functioning digestive, calculative and immune systems.

Picture a special night out on the town. We all merit one of those on occasion and some of us splurge for those even when they're not particularly merited. We are, even on a particularly momentous outing, very often content with the typical three course meal, described in order of presentation as: a starter, the main course and a well-earned dessert. And for our three pack of liquid refreshment, another auspicious line-up might look something like this: a flask of water, a bottle of wine and a double espresso to top things off.

Yes, food and drink: if there are two things that reinforce the comforts and pure delights generated by the most natural offerings of the Law of Thirds, these have to be it. Well, some might say wine, women and song, but that's a subject for another section.

Yes, it is worth noting that not every event or occasion is best marked by allegiance to the Law of Thirds. You may have experienced the extraordinary nine-course meals favored by some Japanese restaurants or a traditional twelve-course meal marking a Chinese wedding banquet, from oysters and sashimi, noodles and rice, to fish, beef, fried croquette, and black sesame ice-cream, and who knows what in between. Don't be fooled. Whether you have six starters, two main courses, and one dessert (or any combination of the three) the normal function of the brain will always re-sort them with the Law of Thirds in mind and reduce the nine, ten or 12 courses into our three basic classifications. Just try to fool the brain. Whether it's red beans, red meat or red rhubarb, the brain will find a place for it.

This is because we like our comfort zones, and most comfort zones are based upon the three common categories favored by no less an authority than Goldilocks: not too little, not too much, but just right.

Okay, okay, so you might go to a better restaurant or a more formal celebration, and a taste of sorbet might interlude the starter and main course to cleanse the palette. A nice touch, no doubt. Some chefs use a simple preparation of fruit or vegetables or soup. Some restaurants often suggest a specific wine or beer to accompany a particular menu item, but the goal is always to lead the diner from one course to the next, not to suggest more courses than there really are.

Did I mention the unfortunate situation that occurs when the wine is served in a bottle as opposed to by the glass? The restaurant may claim a certain reluctance to serve a dish with a certain glass of wine, but the truth is, this is a clever way of strong-arming the customer into buying the entire bottle, a fabulous way for the restaurateur to accrue huge profits, even if it does mean turning you and me into alcoholics.

It is quite acceptable to eschew the comfort of thirds when there are better options available, even if the occasion is rare. Let's look at the contentious and often controversial subject of food labeling to illustrate our point.

Food labeling is both contentious and controversial for many reasons, not the least of which is a lack of consensus as to the best method of presenting important information to your everyday consumer. Some labels highlight five factors, some seven. Some do both. Why is this important in our study of the Law of Thirds? Because these classifications of five or seven or more elements cannot easily be pared down or split to fit the natural function of the brain. And while this might be okay for unwashed windows on the side of a building or the occasional billboard in the middle of no-man's land, it's not a great idea when it comes to our brains and their ability to understand, process and practice. Take a look at our examples below, and see if you can make sense of them.

Yes that's Shakespeare ages of man on the side of a soda can. The calories and sugar pass us by to leave us thinking there is nothing bad inside

You can rest assured that our brains will look at this linear list and settle on three of the elements, though not necessarily the first three, and use those for the purpose of making a nutritional decision. The circle is just confusing, especially if you don't factor in the "per serving" piece at the top of the circle.

How about this one?

This is analogous to looking at a traffic light at a busy intersection, except the lights don't mean what we thought they did, and thus are a tailor-made nutritional fender bender. What does this gaily lit label tell us? Should I eat the bacon roll or run away as fast as my little legs will take me?

We have been given four options to study, discern and decipher. Four is not a good number. Are the bacon roll makers really smart enough to try and fool us? Doubt it. More than likely, our brains are going to use the colors, red, yellow and green to group the information, slice, dice and rearrange the information, and finally to answer the question: to buy or not to buy?

But should we really? Especially knowing that we're clogging our veins with double the Recommended Daily Allowance of all those very unsavory additives. Yes, you caught it: a TLA: RDA.

More than likely, we'll justify our decision for consuming way too much salt, sugar, fat and saturates by saying, "Well, I had to run for the train, I couldn't find a seat, and I'll have to jog all the way to the office." Might as well eat the bacon roll and suffer the consequences.

The same rationalization could apply, now that I think about it, to that special chocolate bar we all crave periodically. Are you really seeking soft nougat and creamy caramel, encased in smooth milk chocolate? Or are you just another cocoa addict seeking your next hit?

So what, you're asking, is the point of this chapter? Well I guess it goes back to the age-old saying, that the customer is always right.

Look at a can of beer, for instance, and you won't see a laundry list of calories and mineral salts mentioned. Well, maybe the calories. But even at that, beer drinkers tend to be content with, at most, knowing at least three of the ingredients – water, barley, and hops – and they're about as natural as you can get.

The point is that you can't force feed the consumer with talk of good health and proper nutrition, and you certainly can't educate them based upon the dietary metrics that are solely important to you. For better or worse, people have to educate themselves based upon their own choices.

It's all about the customer. It's all about communication. It's all about who you're talking to and what you're trying to sell. If you're building a house, sand, cement and water might make a great concrete mix, but if your customer is a house brick, is the brick going to appreciate your communicative charm? Probably not.

"You can lead a horse to water, but you can't make him drink." This is true in particular when you're talking about the things that we put in our bodies. Most people know that a steady diet of cheeseburgers isn't healthy, but if you try and tell them that, you can expect their taste buds to get all excited, and they'll probably just snub their noses at you and head for Burger King.

People have differing ideals. One person's idea of the perfect three-course meal is almost certainly going to be different from the next. People will always live to their own ideals, even if they don't strike us as ideals. Do they really care how much gluten a chocolate bar contains, or are they more interested in how many nuts there are? Do they really care how many calories a steak has, or are they more interested in whether it's rare, medium or well done? Who knows? What is sure is that most of them will live to their ideals whether those ideals are healthy or not.

Sure, not everyone will understand the reasoning behind all of this chatter, but I wonder how many calls or emails Coca-Cola receives each day on the amount of fiber their product contains? I think we can safely say not too many.

Time to study the chocolate bar with a discerning eye – and not all that discerning, to be honest – you'll see that it chooses to display three ingredients not included on the front face of the bar. We probably wouldn't give a second thought to buying the bar if we saw the words: chocolate, caramel and nougat staring us in the face. But for regulatory purposes, as with most other products, the ingredient list is relegated to the back.

Well, some would say, at least they didn't try and hide the ingredients like certain other products we've discussed. Could it be that what's not included is more important to the discretionary values of a chocoholic?

In the end, however, the subject of dining really has little to do with food labeling, calories or healthy choices. In the end, it comes down to the three essential elements of a good meal: the cuisine, the cup and the company.

The Johari Window

Knowledge of what you don't know is just as important as the knowledge that you do know.

Donald Rumsfeld made this statement at a NATO Press Conference in 2002. He said, "Reports that say that something hasn't happened are always interesting to me, because as we know, there are known knowns; there are things we know we know. We also know there are known unknowns; that is to say we know there are some things we do not know. But there are also unknown unknowns – the ones we don't know we don't know."

Whether you are a fan of Mr. Rumsfeld or not, he was, for our purposes, referring, of course, to a Johari Window, a perfect tribute to the Law of Thirds. Here are the three components:

1. The known knowns
2. The known unknowns
3. The unknown unknowns.

The Johari Window applies to just about anything. There are always things that we know about ourselves that no one else does. There are always things that people see in us that we don't see in ourselves. Likewise there are always things that are clear to both ourselves and to others and those very tricky things that no one knows, the unknown unknowns. Sounds like a spy novel, doesn't it.

Put simply, the Johari Window is one of those tools that looks at how we act or behave in any particular social situation, and, if it's used properly will promote successful communication. A very lofty goal, but one we can probably all aspire to.

If you set out on an adventure – let's say a trip to the Amazon rainforest – you can do your research all day long and talk to any number of so-called experts in the field, and still the strongest and most dominant of the three Johari Window components in such a case may turn out to be the unknown unknowns simply because you are setting out for one of those places on earth that is not completely explored, mapped or charted. Does this make for the perfect adventure or just the most dangerous?

Let's assume you're producing a play or directing a movie. Part of the fun is deciding how much to tell your audience and how much to leave up to the imagination. This is the Johari Window in action, but from a different point of view. There are always going to be those things that you and your audience both know (or things you're sharing as well as those things about your subject that he, she, or they in your audience already know). There are those things you know that your audience doesn't (or things you're choosing not to share), and there are those things about what you're communicating that neither of you know (whether it's a lack of information, lack of interest or desire or some other reason).

I love how the Johari Window plays into the arts. We talked earlier about the three-legged stool of creativity? First, you have imagination. Second, you have connectedness. Third, you have desire. Whether the artist has created a painting, a sculpture or a three-stanza-poem, he or she can't possibly know where all the magic and mystery of that creation comes from. Some of this magic and mystery the artist knows and willingly shares with others (the known knowns). Some the artist may know but keeps hidden from his or her audience (or those things that the audience sees in the creation that the artist doesn't). And finally, there will always be things in every artistic endeavor that are completely hidden from both artist and his or her audience (the hidden beauty of the unknown unknowns).

What about war and the Johari Window? That is what Mr. Rumsfeld was, of course, referring to in his quote above.

Just think about it! What can we know about the child who lives through a war? What scars are obvious to us all and what ramifications may never manifest themselves? We know that very little good can come from it. That is the public self. Everyone sees the death and the destruction. But what about the unknown unknowns? What about the scars that are passed on to that child's future generations?

What about the soldier who has, according to the dictates of politicians, been sent to a war to secure the safety of a nation? We see soldiers coming home without limbs. We see soldiers who don't come home at all. These are surely the known knowns. But can we really know about the wounds that soldier's parents carry? Can we know about the loss a community might bear because one man or woman and his or her contribution to that community have been lost forever?

The Johari Window is not just a theory. It is deeply rooted in the Law of Thirds, and therefore it has a profound effect on the workings of our minds. It may not be something we can harness, but it is something we can use to explore more deeply even the most obvious aspects of life.

The Three Appeals

Cover all bases when trying to get your point across.

Aristotle codified how communication should be built for maximum effectiveness by developing his three appeals:

1. Rational appeals
2. Emotional appeals
3. Ethical appeals.

He gave these three very greek names: Ethos, Pathos and Logos.

The rational appeal is a matter of logic (logos). It can also be called a means of persuading others by the use of reasoning. Aristotle being a logic guy, this was, of course, his favorite of the three. The rational appeal is all about giving effective, persuasive reasons and explanations, or elucidations to back up your claims. The facts and nothing but the facts. Hard to lose an argument if you've got the facts to back it up.

Here's an oft-quoted, if slightly embellished, example of this type of appeal: as your teacher, may I say, without beating around the bush, that if you do not do your homework, you will not graduate.

The ethical appeal is really a matter of credibility (ethos). It can also be described as a way of convincing others because of who you are and what you stand for. In other words, you and I tend to believe people we respect. We're products of right and wrong. We want to believe. And if you convince whoever you're appealing to that you're worth listening to, you've just about got them in your pocket.

Twisting the aforementioned example with an eye on the ethical appeal leaves us with: as someone who's been out there in the hard, cruel world, I can tell you that an education is vital if you intend to get anywhere in life, so do your homework.

The emotional appeal is really about appealing to peoples' feelings (pathos). Get them riled up; make them sad; make them laugh; make them feel something. The goal of this appeal is to do whatever it takes to tap the emotional well that lives deep inside all of us. We want to think with our hearts, and if you can tug at someone's heartstrings, you're halfway to the finish line.

Twisting the aforementioned example even further, you have this: as someone who really cares for you and wants you to do well, I really want to encourage you to knuckle down with your school books and make something of your life.

Below is another readily accessible example that comes to us care of journalist and writer Tony Barber, who wrote this piece in his blog regarding a Polish priest who was killed at the hands of the authorities some years back. Take a look:

"A polish priest who was murdered in 1984 by secret policemen working at the time for the ruling Communist authorities was beatified last weekend by the Vatican, a step that puts him on the path for eventual sainthood.

"The news meant a lot to me because, although I'm not Roman Catholic, I came to know the priest well when I lived and worked in Warsaw as a young reporter in the 1980s. "His name was Jerzy Popieluszko, and he was famous throughout Poland for the anti-Communist 'masses for the homeland' that he used to hold at his church."

So how do we look at this three-sentence exposé based upon the theory of the three appeals? In the first sentence, pretty much every word that Mr. Barber uses represents a rational appeal, hard facts that build a persuasive picture and leaves little doubt that there is a concrete and compelling story coming.

The second sentence leans more toward the ethical appeal. Here, Mr. Barber first states his closeness to the victim, and, in one fell swoop, draws your trust by removing religion from his reasoning. Then, he uses this one sentence to build his own credibility by stating indirectly how much experience he has as a journalist. Finally, he adds to the credibility mix by informing the reader that he was in Warsaw at the time and was, in essence, an eyewitness. That's packing a lot of ethical punch into one sentence, thank you very much, Mr. Barber.

The third sentence is an achievement in the use of the emotional appeal. He does this by citing the priest's name, acknowledging his fame, his leadership, and his congregation, and then tops it off by revealing the priest's political clout. Well done!

Such an appeal is undoubtedly persuasive. Could Mr. Barber have chosen a less sledge-hammer approach? Perhaps, but in this case, he chose to go for the jugular and succeeded.

As a side note to the story and a tribute to the Law of Thirds, we should note the three steps to sainthood. The first is to be made venerable; the second is beatification; and lastly is actual canonization.

The three appeals are equally as effective in the art of rhetoric, or what most of us refer to as conversation, oratory or public speaking. Rather than just saying "Hello" or "How are you?" try something more along the lines of, "Hello. It's such a beautiful day, isn't it? It's so good to see you." Rational, ethical, emotional. Toss in the bait, set the hook, reel them in. Aristotle would be proud.

Know this, however. The art of rhetoric is not the just reserve of wordsmiths, orators and liars. Here is an outlandish example of international monetary fund bankers who described the possible default of the Greek economy just recently as "unnecessary, undesirable and unlikely." From Aristotle's point of view, they managed all three appeals in just three un-words.

1. The rational appeal: unlikely
2. The ethical appeal: unnecessary
3. The emotional appeal: undesirable.

Does this make Greece's financial situation any more solid? Does it somehow make their enormous debt less daunting? Well, if you are familiar with the Aristotelian technique in play here, then it's all rather transparent.

The three appeals is a classic example of the Law of Thirds in action; not too much, not too little. We don't want to let our communication efforts get out of whack. Keep them within the realm of thirds, and the mastery of your audience will be appropriate and well-earned. In other words, you're more likely to be heard, your thoughts are more likely to be appreciated, and your company will almost certainly be more desirable to both men and women alike.

The Third Way

Don't just think outside the box. Get into a totally different dimension.

There's always an alternative. There's always a third way. And the third way that we're talking about here is not some amalgam of the other two ways. The third way is a different way.

It's not left or right; it's up. It's not right or wrong; it's different. It's not black or white; it's a color.

In the world of economics, we talk about buying and selling; the third way targets what has become almost a foreign concept in some western countries: savings or storage or accumulation. Saving is very much the same as resisting; resisting the tenets of consumerism and our obsession with acquiring things.

Whatever the term you choose to use, the third way in this arena of thought and economics is called arbitrage; in essence, buy now cheaply and sell when there are more buyers than sellers in the marketplace. Arbitragers are people who buy something in one place and sell it in another, purchase a pair of jeans in Asia, ship them half way across the world (cost circa 50cents) and hopefully sell at a profit, and hopefully pocket the difference. You might think this as being crafty, but, when all is said and done, it's fundamental to capitalism.

Want to arbitrage between the corn price and the price of chickens? Simple, buy the corn and leave with some baby chicks for two months. Crude oil and gasoline, rent a refinery! This, for all intents and purposes, is still arbitrage, but now capitalism is at work and everyone is left applauding your entrepreneurial spirit.

We talk about safe investments versus risky investments, but the third way is to focus on timely investments instead.

If we hold some stock, every day we have three options: we can buy more; we can sell a portion of our holdings; or we can close out our position. There are three questions worth asking in any case. How much? At what price? In what timescale? In essence these options available come at zero cost to us. Therefore a well-timed investment will provide a greater profit than merely a good investment made on the basis of risk and reward.

Moving beyond the world of economics into a world dominated by conflict and resolution, we very often forget the most powerful of forces: hope. Hope keeps us afloat even in the heat of conflict, and hope is the thing that gives power to potential resolution.

In the world of education, we talk about comprehension and befuddlement, but the third way, which is by far the most common way, is the idea of progressing, moving forward, gaining bits and pieces of information. These small steps forward are actually what we call learning.

In the theatrical arts, we talk about comedy and tragedy, when in fact the third way is neither a laughing matter nor a complete disaster. The third way is the common tension of the journey of living day to day, and the very best in stage and screen taps this in such a way that we don't know whether to laugh or cry.

In sports, we talk about winning and losing, which is so incomplete. The third way focuses on competing. It pays homage to showing up and getting in the mix, not just the outcome. Think of the difference.

We can apply the concepts and philosophies behind winning and losing to so many other situations as well. What happens if you end up in the wrong part of town at the wrong time of day and bump into the wrong kind of person? Not a very pleasant scenario for any of us to imagine, let alone face. What are your options? You might fancy yourself taking a stand and going head to head with this nasty fellow, a champion of good against evil. But there is a reality to all such flights of fancy, and, in this case, the truth is that you're far more likely to end up on the losing end of such an encounter unless you turn tail and run as fast as your sneakers will take you. You've heard of the three secrets to avoiding nasty encounters: run, run fast, run faster.

In business, there are three basic approaches to dealing with the inevitable competition that every enterprise faces:

1. You can cast yourself in the role of the attacker, tackling your competition head on and using everything from new product development to price gouging to beat the enemy
2. You can cast yourself in the role of the defender, matching or countering the moves of your competition and hoping to do better, quicker and more effectively

3. You can change directions, broaching other markets or creating entirely new markets.

Life, for all its nuances and idiosyncrasies, is an exercise in problem solving. There are always three considerations when looking at any problem:

1. Which parts of the problem are unlikely to have solutions of any value?
2. Which parts of the problem aren't too serious and can wait?
3. Which parts of the problem are likely to yield the most valuable outcome if solved?

In problem solving, it is often thought that we are most influenced by our perspective and our experience. But there is a third way, and this is based upon the perceived notion of how others will view our decision. Is this a good thing or a bad thing? Or is it a human nature thing, which, in our model would be a third way of looking at the issue, and probably a very insightful way.

We break decision making up into two parts: course of action and outcome. The third way recognizes that neither the strategy nor the end result means a thing without the tactical side of the equation.

What about nature and evolution? Darwin observed the weak and the strong go about their struggle for survival, but concluded it's the adaptability of any species that live on.

Here's a real world example for you. Picture a hostage situation. Picture a police negotiator deciding how to proceed with his or her negotiating strategy. Pleading with the hostage, taking a subservient stance, taking orders is one way. Going in with guns blazing could be a dominant approach, making the orders, saying how it's going to be. But the truth is, it's really the third way – communicating positive elements of love and compassion – that normally proves the most effective way to end a negotiation in the most positive fashion.

Right, left or up. Yes, it's a choice. But it's not simply a matter of being oppositional or adversarial and saying, I'm always going with the third way.

The up alternative is a means of exploring the right way, the most productive way and the most meaningful way.

Life is not, for example, a matter of heroes and villains. It's about doing your work and stepping back. It's about a willingness to give other people credit for the good things and a willingness to accept responsibility when things go awry.

We can talk about leading and following but the third way is much more about inspiring.

We talk about birth and death, but the third way focuses on maximizing the moment, the way you live your life.

Yes, the in vogue phrase for today's in vogue people is to think outside the box. Nothing wrong with that saying or that philosophy; in fact, it can speak directly to the point of our entire discussion. And that is, when you step away from the left and right and delve into completely different dimensions, you'll find the third way a worthy path to travel, not to mention a vital nod to the Law of Thirds.

Three Represents

Virtuous circles spiral outwards.

So what, you are asking, are the Three Represents? Picture a triangle. Picture a problem — any problem — as having three distinct sides, just like our triangle. Each side of the triangle represents a key task that has to be performed to see the problem effectively resolved.

The problem, whatever it may be, cannot be solved solely by the efforts, tools, or people-power represented by just one side of the triangle. The problem needs to pass through and around the triangle to affect a solution. In some respects, it's even better to describe this problem-solving cycle as a circular chain.

In all triangular problem-solving cycles, there will always be one link that is the strongest, and this player, if you will, will, under the most effective circumstances, offer aid, support and backing to the least effective links. And sometimes, the strongest link today will be the link in need of support tomorrow. That sounds a lot like life itself, doesn't it?

Now let's do some digging. The Communist Party of China (represented by the TLA CPC) might be an odd place to go looking for self-supporting and complementary uses of the Law of Thirds, but maybe that's our own single issue prejudices of what the CPC is all about that makes it feel that way. Trust me on this one. This has nothing to do with ideology.

The original use of the term Three Represents was offered by Comrade Jiang Zemin in 2000 when he was trying to sell the concept that the Communist Party really was a party of the people. His Three Represents were, as he put it, a summary of the nature, purpose, and historical tasks of the CPC. Please bear in mind the word tasks, because accomplishing a task is what this is all about. His Three Represents were:

1. The Party must always represent the requirements of the development of China's advanced productive forces
2. The Party must always represent the orientation of the development of China's advanced culture
3. The Party must always represent the fundamental interests of the overwhelming majority of the people in China.

Okay, give Mr. Jiang credit for having a vision and for exemplary use of the Law of Thirds. Not too much, not too little. He could have opted for a nice, clear three word summary: progress, order, people.

However, this conclusion is not, from a worldly point of view, a huge surprise or completely original. Brazil, for example, has the foundation pieces of its philosophy written across its national flag: "Ordem e Progresso." Translated: order and progress. The Brazilians were apparently not as well versed as the Chinese in the use of thirds in making their points – egregiously leaving out the most important component of all: people – and thus demonstrating why they have struggled with social development for so long.

Let's give credit, however, to a number of other countries who have used the Three Represents to rally the masses. Andorra chose a more low-key motto: Virtue, Unity and Strength. In Zimbabwe's "Unity, Freedom and Work" manifesto, the power of a defensive and guiding mantra is not lost. How about France? They coined the phrase: Liberty, equality, fraternity. Interesting how all three are people-related. Good for the French. And my favorite, from Guatemala: grow free and fertile. I invite you to draw your own conclusions.

The beauty of all of these mottos, and many more like them, is that, as we said in our opening paragraph, if one of these pieces is missing or ignored – if the French were to ignore their commitment to equality, for example – the other two pieces will likely fail. Each represents the other, giving support and credence to the whole.

Returning, however, to the author of the Three Represents, Jiang Zemin describes his statement as an extension of Marxism, and, in fact, the tenets are pretty much identical to classical Marxism.

So why, if we skip any pre-conceived ideologies that we may have, does Marxism work, and how does the concept of order, progress and power to the people work collectively?

Remembering our problem-solving triangle, the tenets work in a complementary manner, each reinforcing the next. Order infers that there is a foundation for progress, while power to the people infers that there will be no tendencies toward disorderly behavior and possible revolution. Progress gives the masses more power, which implies more consumption and more happiness, all of which are reinforced by the positive effects of order. In theory, a winning combination.

However, political theory is one thing, while the actions that emerge from the regimes and/or governments charged with ensuring that all three sides of our triangle work in harmony is quite another. In other words, the application of the Three Represents is often far afield of the ideology espoused by the motto.

The spiral of these complementary forces can go either way. On the far extreme, order might be interpreted as oppression. Progress might be taken to mean arming a nation to the teeth. Power of the people might turn out to mean the power of a select few. On the other extreme, order might be a nation with little violence or crime. Progress might refer to a growth of middle-class capitalism. Power to the people might mean an increase of individual freedoms.

We could call these inward and outward spirals. A tyrannical government bent on repression would be an inward spiral. A growing democracy bent on expanding individual freedoms would be an outward spiral. In the first, power turns out to be a dictator who interprets progress as a growing army and an expanding bank account. In the second, power might be free elections and progress might be the ability of a schoolteacher to buy a new car.

Let's return to China, a country growing wildly as far as their economics goes and the expansion of its middle class. Yet it remains, curiously, one of the last bastions of communism. Oh, it's also a country with almost as many bicycles as people, and I will leave it to you to decide whether this is an inward spiral or an outward one. I happen to ride my bike nearly every day, so you can imagine where I come down on the issue. Just slightly prejudice.

And not to segue too far from our points about the Three Represents, let's keep in mind that a bicycle frame is made of three primary tubes, which, in a very symmetrical way, represents the support of the rider and the aerodynamics of the machine. The top tube, or the horizontal one running from the handlebars to the saddle, is subjected to torsional load as the rider pedals along. The down tube running from the handlebars to the pedals is under tension, while the seat tube from the saddle to the pedals is subjected to compression.

The bicycle is, in many respects, a perfect example of the Three Represents in action, albeit an industrial example. Just like the face and the inner-workings of a precision watch, the bicycle frame has benefited from 200 years of evolution and perfection, and the support, balance and symmetry demonstrated by the three primary tubes is nearly flawless.

We can choose to make a bicycle with no top tube, which you see in women's bikes from years gone by, and where the down tube is made larger to handle the increased torsion. Or there are models where the down tube is replaced by a steel cable to cope with the tension. But these are exceptions, and exceptions don't generally carry the day when it comes to the power of the Law of Thirds.

Remembering again our triangle and how it relates to problem-solving, you can see that no one of our three tubes stands alone in its appointed task. The fabrication of the frame – it is no accident that it is a triangle, of course – intentionally distributes the compression, torsion and tension across the bicycle frame, just like the movements of a watch. The more precise the distribution, the better the bike. Each tube represents the other. The various forces are equally complementary.

As with all tasks that we face and all problems that we must cope with, there are complications that change the dynamics of our problem-solving triangle and cause different stresses on each task.

To keep it simple, let's use our bicycle to illustrate. Assume we have a broken joint somewhere along the frame. The frame may still be usable. But the strength exhibited before the damage was done to the frame and when the interaction of the parts was completely complementary is only a fraction of its former self.

What about an example taken from the Green movement? Picture a glass bottle; beer, wine, water or soda, it doesn't matter. Picture this glass bottle moving through the recycling process and you will find three irrevocable links: the bottler, the customer and the recycler.

It is pretty obvious that the entire effort will be negated if the recycling company no longer sends its trucks around to pick up recycled materials from its customers: in our example, the glass bottles we spoke of. Yes, some customers will still load up their cars and take their recycled bottles, plastics and cans to the recycling center, but many won't. Then again, in the recycled paper industry, the price paid by the manufacturer for used paper and cardboard is often negative, but the chain remains intact. In the best-case scenario, virtue is held out by all members in the chain. Someone will always offer to help out: their business is my business.

In the matter of the Three Represents, whether we're talking about tasks on the grand scale of building a political party such as the CPC or something as basic as building a bicycle frame, we always have three complementary forces that can either work in perfect harmony – a rare occasion – or complicate the task to the point of failure. They are: push, pull and oppositional.

The goal of the Three Represents is a burden equally shared. The balance necessary for a well-crafted bicycle frame is easy to understand. When it comes to the Communist Party described by Jiang Zemin, the balance between the concepts of order, progress and the power of the people may be precarious at best, but you can see the beauty of this ideal were it ever to find true balance.

That's the goal of the Three Represents in any aspect of our lives, whether it's a task involving business, community or relationships. It is a joint sharing of responsibilities and a respect for the part each of the three plays in accomplishing the said task. When all goes well, the burden is shared, and the load spreads across the problem-solving cycle that we described earlier as a circular chain. In a perfect world, the forces move outward, dissipating and dispersing as the task nears completion.

Let's take a leap of faith and examine the criminal justice system, which is, believe it or not, constructed much like a bicycle frame. The basic structure of the system is constructed around the three arms of criminal justice: the police, the courts and corrections.

Every criminal – or perhaps it would be better to say, anyone thrust into the system, guilty or innocent – must travel through and around this system, encountering, battling and perhaps defeating one or more of these arms.

In terms of the Three Represents, the police apprehend, the courts sentence and corrections tries to fix. Well, good luck with that, but you see how it works in a perfect world.

If all of the sides of the triangle work in balance and in a complementary fashion, our criminal picks up his or her life, re-enters society, and is no longer a strain on the system. If one side of this triangle fails, the others are weakened and we end up with a whole lot of people contributing nothing to society, but costing society a truckload of money. Not good.

It is important to understand, I think, that as each criminal moves through the system, the load or burden is not reduced, even if the three arms work in perfect harmony. Why? Because as sure as it will rain somewhere in the world today, a new criminal will come along and test the system, adding to the load, straining the frame, and pushing the principals of the Three Represents to the limit. That's called life.

In what we might call a worst-case-scenario, the stress of the system becomes overburdened: the police can't corral all the lawbreakers; the courts can't process them fast enough; and corrections fix fewer and fewer of them. The inner spiral, in this case, spins increasingly out of control, a fracture occurs and a weld cracks. The result is the three hells of anarchy: lawlessness, chaos and revolution.

Let's backtrack once more to our recycling example. Let's take an example of one such recycled material: PET. You got it; another of those damned three letter acronyms. PET, for those of you who may not know, is a consumer plastic often used in making packaging materials such as bottles and containers for everything from soft drinks to detergents.

Let's look at each factor in the life cycle of PET, how each plays a part in the recycling crusade, and how all of this fits the Three Represents model.

First off, we have the manufacturer, or, in the case of the soft drinks we just mentioned, the bottler. They take the raw PET (think of it as common plastic) and form a container. For the sake of this example, we'll use a half liter bottle of a popular cola product. Take your pick.

The manufacturer's responsibility in this task is to construct a bottle that qualifies as safe for use as a cola container while being effectively recyclable as well. Okay, good.

The manufacturing process must also include all the necessary labels informing the consumer of the products' recyclable components; this might be a direct reference to recycling – Please Recycle – or a more subtle, indirect use of that very identifiable recycling symbol; you know, the one with the three arrows connecting in a triangular formation.

The second side of our problem-solving triangle is, of course, the guy or girl who buys the cola, drinks it, and then, if all goes well, drops it in a recycling bin.

Third in the chain is the waste management company. Hopefully, there are receptacles handy, as they are often right next to the vending machine that dispensed the soda in the first place.

You've heard of the Iron Triangle that dominates U.S. politics. That's the three-sided political relationship between Congress, any Federal department or agency, and any particular industry or interest group. It's pretty well understood that as long as the loop between these shakers and movers persists, they will dominate all policy-making in their respective areas of interest, the will of the people and the concerns of the country be damned.

In professional sports, you have the Three Represents formed by the players, the owners and the fans, if only the fans really knew how much power they have.

In the arts, the loop is formed by the artist, the art world and the art lover. In this case, the art lover dictates to the art world, which influences the artist, who puts themself on the line by stretching the imagination of the art lover.

So there is the world of the Three Represents. The hope is that you're not more confused than when you started this section. The Three Represents is a problem-solving device for almost any task. And the idea is that it takes industry, effort and co-operation to get the job done properly. Now let's span the globe and take a look at that select group of people who have mastered the Law of Thirds, or, at the very least, used it in ways that illustrate beyond doubt its exceptional power. Hold onto your hat.

Preamble

So now we have familiarized ourselves with the depth of the Law of Thirds and how the division of threes can be used as a mental tool, as a device to organize our thoughts and as a means of applying consistency and order within our lives.

At the beginning of this book, we contemplated two scenarios that we felt could not be helped by thought or division. They were very much the single issue concerns. The first was our example of the 100-metre sprint. The second revolved around one's response to an incoming missile when on the high seas. And while these are not perhaps what most of us would call everyday occurrences, it turned out that they were, in fact, subject to our discourse surrounded by thinking and division.

Take first our example of the sprinter. Nine-plus-seconds of explosive energy. By definition, not a lot of time to think. And yet we determined that, indeed, thought, planning and execution guide the sprinter through his or her preparation before a race and from beginning to end.

In fact, the next time you're lucky enough to be watching an athletic meet of the highest caliber – the Olympic Games, for instance – I encourage you to pay close attention. Note the athlete's pre-race routine. Note the tuck jumps almost all employ, impressive enough, I dare say, to make a kangaroo proud. Why then this interesting exercise? To stretch? To warm up? In truth, the tuck jump is meant to load the ankle and knees with elastic energy that manifests in an explosion from the starting blocks.

Yes, that is phase one of what is – you guessed it – a three phase race. The second of these three is called the drive. The drive is that calculated and highly practiced process of uncoiling from the crouched and stationary posture in the starting blocks to the upright stance of a sprinter driving toward full acceleration. Once in this stance, one hopes to be ahead, of course, but whether the sprinter is or isn't, he or she implements the third phase of our sprint, called here the stride. Here the sprinter concentrates on keeping the body upright, the arms pumping and the legs fluid, and all attention focused on the finish line. Don't let anyone tell you that the Law of Thirds isn't in play in the life and times of the 100-metre sprinter. For indeed it is.

For our second example – the incoming missile directed at your frigate alone on the high seas – we discover the instantaneous need for thought at its highest level: decision-making. In this case, fight or flight. Let's say that we adopt the premise that facing a problem head-on is better than running away; one decision made. Second decision: how then will we get the job done? Let's say we decide on the so-called three-pronged goalkeeper process. The goalkeeper is, in military terms, a close-in weapon system designed to detect, target and destroy. Hopefully, you have one on the ship we've described in our example.

Whether the incoming target is a 50mm shell, an anti-ship missile or a Kamikaze aircraft, the goalkeeper is a very handy thing to have when the brain chooses fight over flight. Indeed, a weapon system that reacts within seconds might sound complicated, yet we know by this time that implementing a process based upon thirds fills us with calmness and contentment.

So now that we've broached the subject of the goalkeeper process, let's take a closer look at how this system fits in with the Law of Thirds. Prepare to be amazed.

It should come as no surprise to you that accuracy is a key attribute to this system. In order to have any hope of destroying an incoming missile, you better have the accuracy necessary to hit the thing. Pretty crucial. The goalkeeper system depends upon the combination of two RADAR systems: one built for searching, the other designed for tracking. It's also quite handy to have a camera system for operator oversight, but perhaps I'm splitting hairs.

Then come the three vital functions of the systems' ubiquitous computers. Their jobs at this point are to categorize, prioritize and engage the target.

The target is, naturally, engaged with a very high-powered gun. Or, in the case of the British Aircraft Carrier HMS Invincible, three 30 mm, seven-barrel Gatling guns. The rounds are equipped with three highly desirable characteristics: high velocity, high density and high impact capabilities.

Lastly, the system and its three interconnected parts – the tracking radar, the computer system and the guns – are blessed with an exceptional rate of execution. A single direct hit on an incoming missile is, sorry to say, unlikely to be enough to prevent some degree of damage to our ship, so the goalkeeper is blessed with the ability to carry out several hits within a few hundredths of a second. That's not bad shooting.

The entire process can thus be summarized with the following Three Represents:

1. Accuracy
2. Power
3. Impact ratio.

Everything from the goalkeeper's design and engineering to its in-action capabilities are based upon the use of thirds. Even for an apparent single-issue machine, count on the power of thirds to play a part. Powerful, the concept is also logical. Logical, it is also surprising. Surprising, it is also captivating.

What is perhaps even more powerful, more logical and more surprising, is the way we can communicate to others using the Law of Thirds. And once understood, this vehicle of communication will happen automatically. When you or I communicate our message, whether it is instructive, entertaining or informative in nature, and whether it is delivered via the written word, an art form of some type or verbally, the person on the receiving end of that message (or actually their sub-conscious minds) will take more notice. Guaranteed.

You can see it in this last passage. The use of thirds runs throughout, and the effect is unmistakable.

In practice, it might not always be possible to stop and review the list of techniques we explored in our previous pages, nor is the art of thinking on our feet always as easy as we hope it might be.

In our favor, however, is the wonderful, delightful fact that the brain is a most adaptable machine. Want proof of how quickly and seamlessly are brains can become accustomed to thinking in thirds? Just take a moment and tap your imagination. Picture a hole-in-the-wall pub in London where a group of dedicated darts players are gathered. Now watch them calculate their scores. The process is so instantaneous that sometimes we forget that the sport is based upon three darts, three rings within the target and three possible multiples.

Let us spend some time now looking at some examples of the Law of Thirds in action. What better way than taking time to listen to people applying the use of thirds in their own lives?

This is undoubtedly the most powerful form of learning of all, opening ourselves up to the stimulus raining down on us from three distinct sources: people, places and events.

These examples occur in every facet of life, in every profession and without the slightest regard for someone's choice of political party, their favorite color or the size of their waistline. The Law of Thirds has no favorites. All you have to do is look for examples throughout the day and open yourself up to them.

In our case, however, we are using print as our medium and so we're restricted slightly in our choice of examples. Bear with me.

Example one of the Law of Thirds in action: a police inspector talks to the media on the death of a citizen. He says:

"My heart goes out to the family, friends and other people affected."

Now as a police inspector, it's an unfortunate fact of life that such statements are part of his or her vernacular on a fairly regular basis. However, on its own, his quote conveys unmitigated sincerity. He manages this by splitting the group of people affected by the tragedy into thirds – family, friends and others – instead of throwing them all into one impersonal heap.

This method of splitting explanations, descriptions or accounts into patterns of three also serves to diversify a statement while adding poignant details that draw the listeners' attention and holds it. For example, the poor chap in the previous quote might also be described in his obituary this way:

"He was a loving father, brother and son."

"He leaves behind an adoring wife, three loving children and his grieving parents."

What does this use of thirds do? In just one sentence, we now have a sense of a real person with a real life and the real people who will long grieve him.

Now let's turn to the world of professional communicators and how some of them use the Law of Thirds to garner the greatest impact.

Winston Churchill once said, "A politician needs the ability to foretell what is going to happen next week, next month and next year. And to have the ability afterwards to explain why it didn't happen."

Franklin Roosevelt made famous one of the most poignant tributes to the Law of Thirds when he said, "Be sincere; be brief; be seated." You have to love that.

BBC Journalist Pallab Ghosh, a particularly effective speaker, was once interviewed on the topic of the media's coverage of science for the BBC's own NewsWatch program. Here are a couple of extracts.

On the subject of media expertise, Mr. Ghosh said:

"We've got 35 reporters, correspondents and producers specializing in science, health and the environment. And that's the largest concentration of journalists in any newsroom I suspect."

Well done, Mr. Ghosh. He further adds:

"... the BBC is unusual, certainly from a broadcast point of view, in specializing in certain areas. We have home affairs specialists, foreign affairs specialists and health, environment and scientific specialists."

As you can see, Mr. Ghosh splits his teams based upon their roles, but also based upon their specialization. He then uses the Law of Thirds to describe the complete team and elevate them to an even higher level.

The interview continues, and our BBC correspondent carries on to the subject of fact checking. He says:

"It's very rare for things to be written by journalists that are not published in high profile journals such as the BMJ and the Lancet... [But] the editors of these journals perhaps ought to exercise a bit more restraint themselves before deciding to publish studies that are of a low sample size, that don't seem quite right, and that haven't been properly referred."

Here Mr. Ghosh is saying that much material is sourced from specialist publications. He wants to emphasize what is wrong in the world of improper or ineffective fact checking while doing his best not to highlight the actual publications themselves. He therefore does not use three examples to cite offending journals, only two (note how it takes the emphasis off the journals and puts the focus on his commentary). Thinking on his feet, he also wows us by citing the three appeals. Rationality – sample sizes; emotional – bad feelings; and ethical – improper referencing.

He then goes on to comment on conflicting stories. He says:

"Well, judgment is everything; judgment is a thing that specialists at the BBC hope to bring to bear. Sometimes we get it hopelessly wrong. There were parts of the BBC reporting on the Fiona Marr case that I feel personally – you know – was not our finest hour. I think it's a case where there is a body of evidence on one side of the argument, but the other side of the argument seems more interesting. And they're given more prominence."

Mr. Ghosh admits problems, yet he expertly deflects the listeners' attention by using no less than three, yes, I said three word idioms. Although he is saying something went wrong, the mind is completely bamboozled after listening and/or reading the transcript.

He continues by constructing two straw men built from three word idioms once again. He says:

"I think, a while back, not just the BBC, but other media outlets were having climate change skeptics arguing science on an equal par with people who've done a great body of work, where the weight of the evidence suggested a certain thing."

The two straw men are now firmly constructed, even though a climate change skeptic against a bona fide scientist should be a one-sided fight.

Alas, he then enters into a three sentence assault, saying:

"I think, not just the BBC, but all media outlets have learnt that science is different. We can't treat an area that has a weight of evidence with the same equality as a kind of quirky idea put forward by someone who has few, if any, scientific credentials. So we do get that now."

The two straw men start out as equals, but a single "few, if any" idiom is enough to fell the "climate change skeptic" straw man.

Yes, I admit, I turned my so-called preamble into something closer to an amble through the park, but I wanted to illustrate the 'real world' concept behind the Law of Thirds before we jump into even more poignant, daring, and even slightly irreverent examples drawn from the heady worlds of arts, science, politics and business.

So, if you're with me, let's linger no longer.

The Art of Thirds

The term Renaissance, of course, refers to a cultural movement that spanned nearly four centuries from the 14th to the 17th century. It began in Florence, in Italy, and spread throughout much of Europe. The word means to be born again. Therefore, a renaissance is a term used to describe a return to, or a revitalization of, cultural trends from the past.

Fashion trends, as we all know, come and go and often come back again; in other words, certain fashion statements from days gone by come back into style and are once more all the rage. Makes me glad that I held onto my seersucker suit.

You could say that society has a tendency to look back in a nostalgic manner to the ideals of the ancients. This ancient thinking, ancient being a relative term, is then learnt all over again, even if those learning it have no connection whatsoever to the past trend.

This, of course, happens in the world of music all the time. Big band music is suddenly popular again after 70 years in the deep freeze. It happens in architecture as well; tutor, once the standard bearer for homes designed in the early 1900s rises from the ashes and influences architects building homes in the 21st century.

It certainly happens with the art world as well. The modern and the abstract are rejected in favor of classical and realist, which then becomes the popular trend once again.

The Renaissance of the 14th to 17th century actually found much of its inspiration from the Byzantine Period dating back as far as 300 AD. We call that time the Middle Ages. The artistry of the Renaissance can be seen all across Europe, and we can pick from a slew of notable Renaissance artists. There was so much exceptional art created in this period that it is still held up as notable, and, for want of a better expression, not modern.

Hans Memling was one such artist. We know nothing of where he trained, or how he built his reputation, but by 1467, he was accepted to the Bruges Guild of Saint Luke as a master. This got our fine gentleman some much-deserved attention, and leads us to a discussion of art and the Law of Thirds.

Memling's first recorded work is what is known as a triptych. A triptych is a painting created using three separate panels that come together to form one portrayal. The painting in question is titled The Last Judgment. In the center panel, we find ourselves absorbed with a moving depiction of God passing judgment on the souls of men. The left panel illustrates in bold brush strokes God's ascendancy into Heaven. In the right panel, the artist depicts an angel of God scrutinizing the damned as they descend into Hell. This passionate, somewhat disturbing piece now hangs in the Narodowe Museum Gdansk. And while the subject matter is surely a representation of ideals laid out in the Christian bible, it is very much in tune with the Law of Thirds.

Memling's Altar of Passion is a similarly created triptych. In this case, the subject of the crucifixion and resurrection of Christ are painted in rich, evocative colors that expertly draw the eye from panel to panel. In the left, we feel Jesus' pain as he labors under the burden of his cross. In the center, his crucifixion between two common thieves wrenches at the heart. And finally, in the right panel, the celebration of His resurrection. A masterpiece by any standards, but also a fitting tribute to the Law of Thirds.

Triptychs are not the reserve of European Renaissance artists. They can be found in works of Japanese and Chinese painters going back centuries. As we have stated earlier in the book, the Asian world has long been in tune with the division of thirds and a number that cannot be divided by any but itself and the number one.

It is not, however, only in the world of painting that the Law of Thirds is at work. If we look at fields as diverse as architecture and flower arranging, we discover the symmetry of three, also the balance and the calming that this magical number brings. Ikebana, the Japanese art of flower arrangement always emphasizes the three parts of the plant – flower, stems and leaves – and relies entirely on three design elements: shape, line and form.

One of my very favorite works by Vincent Van Gogh, Still Life with Three Birds Eggs, is a more literal use of the Law of Thirds, but there are multiple uses all within one extraordinary work. For one, there are three birds' nests side by side. Secondly, there in the clutches of the third nest are three eggs. And finally, each of the three nests is illuminated under three distinct levels of natural light. A most pleasing work!

Paul Gaugin works the same magic with his 1888 Still Life with Three Puppies. It is a marvel in the use of threes. His three puppies are drinking water from a bowl, while in the foreground our eyes are drawn by three clay goblets and an arrangement of three pieces of fruit. Delightful!

Look deeper at many compositions, especially paintings from the Renaissance and pre-Impressionism, and we often discover another cliqued troika:

1. Birth or renewal.
2. Beauty or life
3. Decay or death.

But this oft used and often-overused trio finds meaning in some of the Renaissance era's finest religious triptychs. The ones we recognize most readily are the many depictions we see of the Holy Family: Jesus, Mary and Joseph. A common theme would be birth as represented by Jesus, beauty as represented by Mary, and decay or death represented by Joseph in his frail, declining years.

But let's be honest, triptychs are not the first thing that comes to mind for most of us when we're thinking about the great painters of our time, our good friend Van Gogh among them. Ask a hundred people to list the three subjects that pop into their heads when they think about good, solid oil painting and you're likely to hear:

1. Your classic bowl of fruit
2. Your even more classic vase of flowers
3. Your standard reclining naked woman.

It's from these three winners that Van Gogh chose to make his contribution to history. No, not the naked woman with baby and skull and any other reclining naked women. Not that he didn't paint women and paint them well. His subjects were a bit unusual: a widowed first cousin; a prostitute named Sien; shy spinster; and a seventeen-year-old peasant girl. No, I'm talking about his desire to introduce to his paintings two new pigments: chrome yellow and Prussian blue. So what was it going to be? A bowl of lemons or a pitcher of summer sunflowers. Fortunately, he chose the sunflowers, and the result was one of the most sought after paintings in history.

Interestingly, our genius Frenchman did actually paint lemons. Three lemons, five lemons, and 13 lemons on a plate. All prime numbers.

But birth, beauty and death are difficult to portray with lemons, aren't they? So Van Gogh found more expressive combinations: sunflower buds bursting with life, bright and beautiful blooms, dead and lifeless seed heads; yellow flowers, green stems and blue table clothes.

Van Gogh understood the intricacies of painting with oils. But he also understood the Law of Thirds as a means of integrating the power of communication into his work. Combining the two turned a great technical artist into an even greater painter.

Want to up your game? Then I suggest you do the same. Take your skills, in whatever area you are most strong (or most deficient) and assimilate the Law of Thirds into your thinking. Let it happen naturally. Trust your instincts. Van Gogh did. It's too bad he died before people like you and I understood his genius.

So what about sculpture? Sculpture is, in fact, the quintessential expression of three dimensional artwork. We think of shapes created by marble and glass. We think of objects built from wood and metal. But in fact, there are three main types of sculpture. Not surprising. We call them: assemblage, in-the-round and relief.

In-the-round is what we usually think of when we talk about sculptures, those free standing pieces surrounded on all four sides by empty space and generally made from one material. Assemblage is similar to an in-the-round sculpture, only it's made from an assortment of objects or material. A relief is a form or picture that projects out from, or is mounted on, a vertical surface.

Interestingly, the term sculpture has lately been extended to works featuring three complementary elements previously reserved for music, writing or theater. These are sound, text and light, and when brought together in something as aesthetic as a water fountain, the effect can be magical.

And then there are sculptures that move, like hanging mobiles. You could define sculptures that move by the three basic functions of movement: motion, balance and co-ordination. Story telling is probably the earliest art form, and surely an outlet for our imagination that most of us thrive on. Whether it was Cro-Magnon man spinning stories in his cave, or fishermen exaggerating about the one that got away, this was and always will be a form of art benefiting from the use of thirds.

Although guys like Aesop and the Brothers Grimm were prolific writers, it's interesting how we best remember those stories with three characters: The Three Black Princesses; The Three Green Twigs; The Devil and the Three Golden Hairs. All classics.

How about Disney? The Three Caballeros; The Three Musketeers; The Three Little Pigs. Classics as well! And of course, Mickey Mouse only had three fingers. Obviously, somebody in Disneyland was clearly using the natural process of the brain when he or she came up with Mickey.

Some of our most classic books and movies tapped into the Law of Thirds to produce titles that are as memorable as they are lasting. Tell me you don't remember Three Billy Goats Gruff, Three Blind Mice, or the infamous Three Stooges.

Goldilocks – what a great story – may have utilized the Law of Thirds with as much finesse as any: three beds, three bowls of porridge, three chairs, and of course the three bears, all forming the idealized trinity of a family.

How about the ever popular movie trilogy or the art of splitting the story across three motion pictures? It's the three point turn of the film world. If the first movie is a flop, it gives you an opportunity to come up with something else the next time around (assuming the studios are willing to fund you). Of course if the first film is a blockbuster, you can pretty much write your own ticket on films two and three.

Pick your poison. I'm a huge fan of Ridley Scotts' Alien Trilogy. But you've recently been bombarded by The Lord of the Rings Trilogy. We had poltergeists, cyborgs and robocops. We've had rush hour, teenage mutant ninja turtles and Die Hard. Trilogies cover all genres.

But perhaps the most famous and most long-lasting is George Lucas' Star Wars Trilogy. And within the trilogy were numerous uses of the Law of Thirds. We had three heroes: Luke, Lea and Han. We had an inferred love triangle. We had three of the most famous humanoid-like characters ever created: the eccentric and clumsy C-3PO, the lovable and unflappable R2-D2 and the enigmatic and charming Yoda. Aristotelian rhetoric immortalized in fantasy? Sure. Why not.

But Star Wars wasn't the first film to win us over with just-this-side-of-human characters. How about the Wizard of Oz, the 1959 classic. Remember the Tin Man, the Cowardly Lion and the Scarecrow? And how about the unforgettable three word defense mantra delivered by the Cowardly Lion: "Put 'em up, put 'em up, put 'em up."

The Wizard of Oz, you might remember, was one of the first films ever filmed in color. They called it three-strip technicolor. No, it wasn't the first. In fact, you can go back to the 1930s when Disney produced Donald Duck in color, and The Three Little Pigs, which was probably the earliest popular technicolor film, a 1933 production feat. Of course, the pigs were also the characters who went up against one of the best known of all bad guys: the Big Bad Wolf. You can call that a mantra or you can talk about a three-legged stool. But either way, it's compulsive viewing at its best.

If this sounds all a little too antiquated, we can take a dangerous leap into the present day and touch on the various outlets for art and entertainment currently consuming us.

From film to television we go, remembering a semi-popular game show called Win, Lose or Draw, with rules much like those of truly popular games like Pictionary or Charades, but it didn't last very long. Apparently, audiences didn't get much joy out of a show that so often ended in a meaningless draw. Clearly, they didn't understand or appreciate the Law of Thirds.

Game shows work very much according to the Law of Thirds. The strength of the show is built on three components:

1. Audience interaction
2. Contestant participation
3. Emotional involvement.

The game show host plays upon these relentlessly. Remove one of three and the show fails. Try to make it too involved or too complicated and you lose most of your audience.

And if a game show doesn't prove to be your cup of tea, then let's take the popular genre of talent contests. The most popular play upon the Law of Thirds in the most obvious, but effective ways. Take American Idol or So You Think You Can Dance. You set the stage with three judges, the optimum number. You always end with the final three contestants. Three allows for a choice without taxing the viewers' attention span or intelligence level; three also allows for enough conflict to avert any lapses into boredom.

However, the most real and important application of the Law of Thirds in these contests is the scoring system. In this day and age, the age-old clap-o-meter has been replaced by voting via phone and text messaging. It's simple, and the audience participation is a huge boon for television ratings. The three pronged voting system works this way:

1. The audience scrutinizes the contests and casts their votes
2. The network tallies the vote (in some cases adding it to the vote of the judges)
3. The vote is announced to great fanfare and increased television ratings.

But this newly devised voting system in which the audience all across the nation is fully invested doesn't determine a winner immediately. No, the voting week to week is only a way of ranking contestants and sending the least desirable, least talented, or least controversial – another pertinent example of thirds – packing. This builds excitement, viewer loyalty and leads to the crescendo of what's known as the last three contestants standing.

But here's the beauty of it. Each week, you not only have the three highest scores, but the three lowest scores. This is the perfect number to instill drama into the event without taxing the viewers too severely. Ah, television! What an invention!

It is this translation from performance to scoring that the viewer finds enthralling. It is very much the same with karaoke scoring. Yes, I know this is a leap of faith, but stay with me. Although listening to someone of less than professional talent sing may or may not be enjoyable, it is the scoring and the guessing of the score that is amusing. How well did your friend perform? How badly did he or she offend the audience? How much laughter did they generate? It's all fun, of course, but people are obsessed with performance and scoring, and they love looking at the podium that places the winner just a little higher than the second place finisher, who is just a tad bit higher than the bronze medalist.

So whether we're digging into the past and exploring the obscurities of Hans Memling or watching a game show that tests your memory or your patience, we see that the Law of Thirds makes its presence felt in almost all areas of art as clearly as it does the fickle art of living.

Most important is the discovery that the most appealing art may also be the most disturbing, and the most gratifying might be the simplest. There are no set rules when it comes to the appreciation of art. The Law of Thirds isn't manipulative when it comes to the arts, but serves rather as a powerful tool for both the creator and the observer.

Necessity: The Mother of All Invention

According to his autobiography, inventor Nikola Tesla had a rather addictive personality; he was obsessed with things like cleanliness and hygiene and was an animal lover who was incessantly drawing pigeons. Of course, you can say that most inventors probably have addictive personalities, be it gambling, coffee, or single malt Scotch, and it is probably a beneficial trait in enduring the trials and errors of invention.

My favorite story about Tesla is that he was further obsessed with the number three and would never stay in a hotel room unless the number was divisible by three. Good for you, Niko.

Tesla didn't exactly invent the electric motor, but he did design the first practical system of generating and transmitting alternating current (AC) for electric power. Digressing slightly, I think it is necessary to note that 'motors' had long before been invented by the time Tesla came around. In fact, the very simplest conceptual motors were nothing more than a magnetic compass-type apparatus and compasses had been in existence for several millennia by the 19th century. It can be said that motors were rarely used outside of the science laboratory in Tesla's time, even though motors adaptable to commercial use were starting to appear.

So the concept of a motor was something Tesla would have been quite familiar with. Perhaps a modern-day analogy would be 3D movies or video phones. A technology well recognized, if yet to be perfected, you might say.

In 1875, Tesla was introduced to the Gramme ring machine. When a professor of his named Jakov Poeschl first demonstrated the machine to Tesla, the motor sparked badly. The part causing the sparks was called the armature, and Tesla postulated that it was possible to actually run the motor without armatures.

Now remember, the first electric motors had two, four or more sets of windings. The Gramme machine itself had 30 coils. By overlaying the alternating current from each coil, a smoother DC (or direct current) can be generated, but people didn't know this back then.

Remember further that this is a book about the Law of Thirds, and when you think about the electric motor, you need to think in thirds. First of all, three-phase electric power is the most common method of AC electric power transmission. It is the most common method used by electric power distribution grids worldwide to distribute power. Got that?

Furthermore, in a three-phase system, three circuit conductors carry three alternating currents, (of the same frequency) which reach their instantaneous peak values at different times.

Then there is the three-phase load. In any motor, the loads must be connected to all three phases of the supply, and the most important class of three-phase load is the electric motor.

Guess who figured this all out, more or less? That's right. Niko Tesla. Tesla had a visual brain that thought instinctively in thirds. He had an eidetic (or photographic) memory. Combined with his ever-addictive attributes, his brain set to work playing with the notion of an armature-less motor. Tesla knew there would be a solution; his instincts told him so.

Let's look at the problem Tesla was faced with. A wire carrying an electrical current, when placed in electrical field, will produce a force tangential to the power of two. We've come across that concept before: the left and right, the backward and forward, and the up and down.

But that's not what Tesla needed. A motor must produce rotational energy; in a similar way in which a steam engine translates air pressure into the linear movement of a piston, which attaches to a crankshaft and turns it.

By any measure, solving this problem would be commercially lucrative, very lucrative. Electricity, after all, was being unwrapped and making its way across America.

Tesla, or rather his amazing brain, eventually came up with the goods in 1882. He filed the patents for a complete electrical production, distribution and manufacture of the contactless AC motor. This was one of nearly 300 patents filed by the man.

The original purchaser of Tesla's patent was Westinghouse, and the foundation of his discovery lives on even today. Three-phase motors are still around today. Three-phase power is to be found in every machine shop around the world. Three-phase generators are at the heart of every power plant, from the original installation at Niagara Falls to the nuclear power plants we see cropping up. Not surprisingly, Westinghouse remains the largest installer of these systems worldwide. The same goes for wind turbines now growing in popularity.

Just look around you. There are endless examples of how linear action is translated into rotational action. A most mundane, but appropriate example? How about the screw top on a milk or drinks bottle. It has three threads. All that's required is a firm grip of your finger and thumb. But the finger and thumb don't rotate; they move past each other in a linear fashion. The result? Even a child can open a bottle in one action; the cap turns a mere 120 degrees, and you're all set.

How about this one? A revolving door! That wonderful invention that is so much more entertaining than the boring hinged variety. We're all familiar with the four-winged version of the revolving door. This clunky, ubiquitous design is most often found in skyscrapers and office towers, there to form an important pressure barrier to prevent updrafts inside the building. Push, and the door rotates. Simple. Tesla would surely have been proud.

On the other hand, maybe you've come across the two-winged versions, more popular in supermarkets and hotels where luggage or grocery carts are more easily maneuvered though them.

You'll have noticed with the two-winged design that it is flawed and nearly as boring as a hinged door, in particular because of the void at the end of each wing. What to do? In a hotel, this annoying void might be occupied by a potted plant or an ornamental arrangement of flowers. A supermarket almost always uses the space for advertising purposes, announcing special offers and the like, a showcase if you will.

But alas, we come to the three-winged revolving door. With three wings – a perfect balance between the clunky four-winged and the insubstantial two-winged design – you have something far more appealing and clearly more conducive to the natural function of the brain.

The three-winged revolving door is a thing of beauty to be sure. And whether you are escorting someone in a wheelchair, pushing a grocery cart, or pulling a suitcase, they are indisputably the most convenient. They appeal to our brains. They satisfy our practical requirements.

A wise man named Tim O'Reilly once said, "An invention has to make sense in the world it finishes in, not in the world it started."

In our world – in the world as seen through the eyes of our naturally functioning brains – the inventions that make the most sense work within the rules created by the Law of Thirds. They make the most sense. They perform. They adapt.

Art of Management

You've probably heard this quote from management guru Peter Drucker: "Efficiency is concerned with doing things right, Effectiveness is doing the right things."

I love this quote for its general mood, but it fails to address the three keys to effective management:

1. Resiliency: defined as the ability to work with adversity in such a way that one comes through it unharmed or even better for the experience
2. Flexibility: defined as the ability to change direction without losing momentum or compromising your purpose
3. Adaptability: defined as the ability to assimilate when necessary, resist when called for, and adjust when it serves the end result one is seeking.

Without these in this ever-changing business environment, you can never master the art of management.

Pick up any business magazine or peruse any financial newspaper, and it's a pretty safe bet that you'll read about a CEO refocusing their company around a three pillar strategy, systems, service and technology; or a three step process, identify, develop and manage; or maybe even the three pronged assault, target, acquire and restructure. All sound pretty impressive, especially since we're already in tune with the natural thought process of the Law of Thirds.

Let's dig out an example and probe a commercial product that most of us might consider mundane, humble, or undistinguished, if only by the fact that the company and its product aren't on every billboard or taking up space on the television. And yet it is, I assure you, a company and a product quite distinguished in terms of a living, breathing tribute to the Law of Thirds.

Not everyone has heard of Nespresso. It is an arm of the food giant Nestlé. Nespresso has over 200 shops worldwide. Except they're not so much shops as they are boutiques, which is exactly how Nespresso advertises their stores: boutiques that take coffee and make it into an exceptional experience. I consider my cup of coffee in the morning an exceptional experience in any case, so Nespresso didn't have to work very hard to convince me.

Nespresso takes the traditional retail experience and twists it into something special, something their CEO, Richard Giradot, calls a trilogy concept. This trilogy concept is what we have been referring to in this book as the Three Represents.

In this case, the first of these Represents is essentially the retail side of the business: part high-end walk-in store, part sophisticated internet experience and part personalized telephone communications.

The second Represent is the exclusive, high-end coffee machines that are the signature pieces of the company. These are specialized machines designed to brew espresso from the contents of the company's pre-made coffee capsules or pods. With an emphasis on precision engineering and stylish design, these are the kind of machines that turn an ordinary kitchen into a gourmet experience. And the key is that high-end doesn't mean way out of my budget.

The third Represent is, of course, Nespresso's coffee itself. With more varieties than your neighborhood Starbucks, attention is shifted from judging the product on taste, to a more harmonious metrics such as origin, roasting, blending and aromatic characteristics. Each coffee comes in a pre-made pod that fits right into the machine and, like magic, delivers a perfect blast of caffeine. I can taste it right now.

These Three Represents create a powerful, yet uncomplicated paradigm of business success; just look at Nespresso's balance sheet. The personal service that comes with the retail side of this paradigm provides essential feedback and an educational mechanism to the engineering arm of the company as well as to the guys and girls creating the blends of the coffee. What a job.

As with all effective Represents, each arm of the collaboration strengthens the whole while supporting the next. If there were less than three aspects to this paradigm, there would be insufficient support. If there were more than three, the strength of the paradigm would be weakened.

So there we have it: the virtuous circles of the Law of Thirds found in a coffee cup. It's a beautiful thing, and so easy for the natural process of the brain to understand, process and appreciate.

Let's stick with our coffee example and travel back to our first chapter where we introduced the concept of the single-issue machine. Consider, in this case, the single issue supply chain where a buyer snaps up all the beans from local growers in a ruthless cost-driven operation, and our brains observe a situation that is clearly unsustainable. Something has to give. Monopolies and a lack of respect for your industry sources is a recipe for disaster. A lack of competition, in this case, will invariably lead to the introduction of either new buyers or fewer sellers. That is the problem when a situation lacks Three Represents. It leads to one or more of the three constants of imbalance: chaos, stagnation and revolt.

But how might this work with regard to our study of the Johari Window? Let's say we have a coffee salesperson. Now juxtapose that against the coffee buyer who represents the salesperson's most important client.

We can see how they fit into the Johari Window below.

	Salesman knowns	Salesman known unknowns	Salesman unknown unknowns
Client knowns	A given	3.	2.
Client known unknowns	1.	Nobody has the answer	You don't have any answers
Client unknown unknowns	Don't tell the client!	Black hole	Blacker than black hole

Goodness! That's nine things to worry about! That is a lot of balls to juggle, even for a salesman. But we're smart enough, given our newfound knowledge surrounding the Law of Thirds to apply the winner's logic to this apparent dilemma and to create a more workable win-win situation for both. How is that, you say? By eliminating the fourth, dropping the fifth, and forgetting the sixth. In so doing, we're left with three soft-cell action steps:

1. Tell the client the answers to his or her questions even before they ask
2. Listen for the unknown unknowns from the client and make them knowns
3. Discover the things you need to find out from the client by being proactive.

Simple, huh? We've moved away from the hard sell, and business is far better for it.

You may not have heard of Nespresso before this enlightening session, but there is little doubt that you're familiar with one of the most successful software companies in the world, the brain child of Paul Allen and Bill Gates that we have come to know as Microsoft. Let's have a peek.

No, I promise not to bore you with the history of this corporate giant, but those of us of a certain age will remember, even without the history lesson, that it all started out as a single product known as DOS. This TLA stands for Disk Operating System, and it was the foundation of the Microsoft empire. But DOS was not enough on its own to defeat all comers, and there were a lot of comers once the term 'personal computer' entered the lexicon.

The lucrative world of personal computer software attracted three imperturbable entrepreneurial types: those with robust minds, innovative outlooks and strong stomachs of risk. The easiest way in the world to be swept away by this wave of entrepreneurial spirit was to get caught flatfooted and standing still.

Not Microsoft. They needed to go beyond DOS, and they needed to do it quick. Their competitors were already hooked into the secrets of DOS and using it as a springboard into other arenas. And everyone was looking for a competitive edge. WordPerfect, for example, was quickly gaining a foothold with such traditional word processors as Wang. So what did Microsoft do? They combined DOS with their Windows software and made them uniquely compatible with the word processor.

Building these three defensive layers, as I like to call them, defined what we think of today as Microsoft. WordPerfect could not run on Windows, but people wanted a Windows system with first rate writing and editing software. Whether you owned a Macintosh or an Atari, the demand was right there at their fingertips. Behold, Microsoft Word. This brash, new software quickly gained ground and overtook WordPerfect; in fact, smashed it to pieces.

All WordPerfect could do was release a Windows version of their software, but it had little chance of success. Aside from the myriad of technical and operational compatibility issues it faced, its biggest and most insurmountable hurdles were the three lines of defense that Microsoft had built into the working model. Behind Word sat Windows: behind Windows sat DOS. The process of installing DOS, then Windows, then Word gave Microsoft's customers – users as they came to be known in the industry – a comfortable, contented, superior feeling. Yes, you heard it: three traits of the snooty Microsoft aficionado.

Still, Microsoft refused to stand still. They were corralling customers who were becoming more and more reliant on their cascade of products. Then came Microsoft PowerPoint, Microsoft Excel, Publisher, Outlook and Front Page, all bent on forming an office suite without peer. In fact, that's exactly what they called it: Office.

But alas, the sharp amongst you will cite that Microsoft has only gone sideways for some years now. Truth be told, the company's share price peaked in the previous century!!! What went wrong, we might ask?

Hindsight gives us an unfair edge on analyzing the state of operations, but that's not about to hold us back. Could it have been data overload? Could it have been force-feeding us new and improved operating systems with fancy names like XP, Vista, and Live? Could it have been that annoying talking paperclip? Or could it have been the lawyers who filed the anti-competition lawsuits against the company that is preventing the Office guys and girls from interacting with the Windows guys and girls in their pursuit of software domination?

It could well be a case of the lawyers weakening the joints of the metaphorical bicycle frame that Microsoft had clearly built over the years. Remember our bicycle example in the chapter on the Three Represents? One flaw in the frame and the perfect combination of balance, support and symmetry is broken. Could that be today's Microsoft? Say it ain't so!

If we study the corporate accounts of Microsoft today, we are drawn to five distinct segments.

1. Client (Windows)
2. Server (Windows for servers)
3. Online (Search/Advertising)
4. Business (Office 2010)
5. Entertainment (Xbox).

Earlier, we talked about the number five in the chapter of the same name. As we said, our amazing brains have a way of sorting through the jumble that so often accompanies lists or subdivisions of five, knowing that the information will be more pertinent in the long run if the list is reduced to three.

It is a matter of information overload on the one hand, but also an excess of information on the other. The mind takes what it needs and moves on. Very efficient.

So how is this 'excess' in the Microsoft product mix contributing to its stagnation? Are there virtuous relationships to be found in this mix that a casual investigation might miss? Does playing Xbox on a Saturday night, for example, make you more likely to employ an exceptional PowerPoint presentation on Monday morning? Or will your skills with Excel drive you to use Microsoft's Bing search engine to find a new pair of sneakers this weekend?

Your own answer is evidence enough for me, but we've seen this ever since man adopted the mistaken belief that more is always better. More is always better as long as more is not more than three.

If you think this is all some sort of newly invented management style, then I'll give you something even older than a 14th century Renaissance masterpiece. Behold Ancient Rome.

Ancient Rome was all too familiar with the Law of Thirds. We have already seen how the three appeals – rational, emotional and ethical – were discovered and codified by Aristotle way back then, and how these three appeals have been influencing everything from communications to the arts ever since.

A tresviri is a group of three people, much as a triumvirate is Latin for three men. In our continuing visitation to the distant past, a tresviri may well have referred to three commissioners who may have been responsible for everything from prison regulation to banking oversight. Why three? For three very good reasons.

1. First, it relieved any single member from having complete responsibility for anything. Ah, the bane of the committee
2. Second, it allowed each member to focus on their specific roles rather than the personalities of the individual themselves. A nice defense against retribution
3. Third, it provided each member with someone to point the finger of blame at without alienating himself completely from the third member. That way nothing really ever got done.

In December of the year 60 BC, Julius Caesar was elected as a consul to the Roman Senate. A year later, he was already unpopular, winning many enemies even as he built a base of power. Caesar was a smart guy. He knew he needed to take the focus off himself and his penchant for rebel rousing and redirect it elsewhere. You guessed it! He formed a defensive pact with two other rather wealthy and influential chaps named Gnaeus Pompey Magnes and Marcus Licinius Crassus. This newly formed triumvirate not only served to increase Caesar's standing, but it insulated him from some of those who were out to get him.

What happened next is probably best left as a warning: that defending the indefensible will only put off the inevitable. Or in Caesar's case, assassination; death by blade, a very unpleasant way to die. Or as Caesar put it: "Et tu, Brutus."

That was only one of Caesar's famous three word mottos, better known as a tricolon. Perhaps an even more profound contribution to his literary legacy was the unforgettable: "Veni, Vidi, Vici." What, you say? Sounds familiar. And so it should, "I came, I saw, I conquered."

Yes, this was also part of Caesar's indefatigable management style. Caesar was not only smart, he was calculating. He didn't pursue the power of an empire without a definite plan. And, in fact, his was made with a keen eye on the Law of Thirds and was based upon three consummate goals.

1. First, he intended to suppress by whatever means all armed resistance in the many provinces of the empire, thus restoring order if not civility
2. Second, he planned to initiate a strong central government in Rome from whence his empire could be easily controlled
3. Third, he had the lofty goal of knitting together the entire empire into a single cohesive unit dominated by one of the greatest armies of all time.

You can admire the management style of Caesar. You can be inspired by the evolution of the vast Microsoft empire. Or you can learn from the well-ordered plan of a company like Nespresso. But what is most viable among these lessons is that success follows a plan based upon thirds, and decline and stagnation are the results of stepping away from the Law of Thirds and believing you can rise above its tenets.

Which inspires me to leave you with a three word motto of my own:

Audio, video, disco. (I hear, I see, I learn.)

Those who have not mastered the Law of Thirds

It doesn't always work, of course.

All along, we have been discussing the power of thirds and how our brains naturally gravitate toward the Law of Thirds.

I think it would be helpful to look at the other side of the coin and explore some pertinent examples of when:

1. The obvious advantages of the use of thirds are ignored
2. Someone thinks they are better than the natural order of things
3. When ignorance or incompetence trump common sense.

No, it is not a coincidence that I happened to tap the Law of Thirds in describing its misuse. What better way to make a point?

Stupid is as Stupid Does

In America, for example, when things go awry, count on everyone to blame the three obvious culprits: the economy, the Government or Hollywood.

In Britain, for another example, when things go awry, count on the people to blame the three usual suspects: everyone but themselves; everyone who is successful; everyone they voted for.

Naturally, the real bad guys in this equation can be described by citing the three stumbling blocks of self-interest: egoism, narcissism and self-absorption. Self-interest is the underlying cause of a problematic British society. Or, as the masses like to say, a distinct lack of respect for everyone and everything.

Oh, most certainly this disease of self-interest can be unearthed in a broad and vast spectrum of areas, organizations and institutions, but high on the list are the Civil Service and the Foreign Office.

Let's use an example that would be laughable if it weren't so embarrassing and sad. The Pope, high commander of the Roman Catholic Church, was coming to town (can London really be called a town?), and the high-minded of the Foreign Office were charged with the task of making the visit a tour de force. Or, at the very least, something less than a total disaster.

The planning began with an intense brainstorming session regarding where the Pope would go, what he would do, and how it would probably make for several very unpleasant days for the guys and girls in the Foreign Office, all of whom despise unpleasant days.

The session delivered an awe-inspiring list of things to do. And of course, we have already discussed how amnestic a list can make us feel; talk about being overwhelmed; or maybe the term was somnolent, because an awful lot of people clearly went to sleep on the job.

What made it worse was the rather thoughtless, disrespectful and sarcastic way in which this so-called list was written, discussed and disseminated. Not a good idea if it happens to leak to the public.

There is a saying in journalism: if you don't want something to appear in the newspapers, don't think it, say it or do it. These folks in the Foreign Office did all three. Yes, the Law of Thirds can come back to bite you if you don't use it properly.

For the curious, you can find the entire list well documented on the internet; it is not worthy of recollection here.

The leaked list clearly demonstrates how using brainstorming as a tool of thought is not only extremely ineffective, but also dangerous to the point of destroying careers.

Brainstorming is based upon three indigenous flaws. The idea is this: rather than getting bogged down in the judgments, personal criticisms and ego-clashes that accompany the ownership of, or the investment in, certain ideas presented by the individual, the team acts collectively. This means there can be no responsibility, accountability, or blame because no one is responsible, accountable, or culpable. If you ask me, bad business right from the start.

Take a look at the statement made by Francis Campbell, Britain's ambassador to the Holy See after the brainstorming list was uncovered by the news media.

"This is clearly a foolish document that does not in any way reflect either the UK Government or the Foreign Office's policy or views. Many of the ideas in the document are clearly ill-judged, naïve and disrespectful. The text was neither cleared nor shown to ministers or senior officials before circulation.

As soon as senior officials became aware of the document, it was withdrawn from circulation.

"The individual responsible has been transferred to other duties. He has been told orally and in writing that this was a serious error of judgment, and he has accepted this view. The Foreign Office very much regrets this incident and is deeply sorry for the offence that it has caused. We strongly value the close and productive relationship between the UK Government and the Holy See and look forward to deepening this further with the visit of Pope Benedict to the UK later this year."

The statement starts by describing the document using just a single adjective, in this case: foolish. This is a clear-cut example of insufficient data. Rest assured that anyone who read the statement was quickly using the Law of Thirds to add to the description. I myself thought: foolish, blundering and bigoted.

Then the mistakes against the Law of Thirds just continued to pile up. The statement mentions two inadequate pairings: the UK Government and the Foreign Office; and then, policy and views. The reader, as before, is left to add to the pairs, which only goes to cloud the statement even further.

Next we see three points of rhetoric: ill-judged, naïve and disrespectful. Okay, that might be seen as a plus, except the author fails to maximize the three appeals by failing to include an emotional appeal.

1. Ill judged (rational)
2. Naive (rational)
3. Disrespectful (ethical).

Furthermore, we see that the individual shouldering the blame was told "orally" and "in writing." Again, the inadequate use of two; clearly the reader is waiting for a third admonishment. I would have liked: orally, in writing and sent packing.

Furthermore, we see the use of a four-word idiom: serious error of judgment. Either dispense with the word serious to form a nicely phrased three word idiom, or punch up the descriptive passage using the Law of Thirds, i.e. a serious, frustrating and botched error of judgment.

Then we see another lackluster use of twos when they express their regrets and how deeply sorry they are. Please. Does that sound sincere to you?

And finally, they fail to adequately describe the relationship between the United Kingdom and the Holy See when they merely cite two less-than-moving points: close and productive, both rational appeals that just don't cut it.

Okay then. Now let's rewrite the statement applying our knowledge of the Law of Thirds.

"This is clearly a destructive, ill-conceived and foolish document that does not in any way reflect the views of my department, the Foreign Office or the Government. Many of the ideas in the document are clearly ill-judged, hurtful and disrespectful. The text was not shared with, reviewed by, or cleared by senior officials before circulation. As soon as senior officials became aware of the document, it was withdrawn from circulation."

So what have we done? First, we let the audience know that the document was far more than just foolish. It was as ill-conceived as it was destructive. By replacing naïve with hurtful, we effectively exchange one of the rational appeals with an emotional one. Note the added power.

We then expand the most offensive pairs with manageable, pointed thirds, and eliminate redundancies by paring down a two here and there with a single point.

The second half of the apology, as all ingenuous apologies do, places the blame for the brainstorming list on a single scapegoat. This proves ineffective because the statement unknowingly represented the triad of parties responsible in the very first sentence. So while the statement tries to implicate the individual responsible, the Foreign Office would have been better served taking ownership.

"The Foreign Office very much regrets this error of judgment and is deeply sorry for the offence which it has caused. We strongly value the relationship between the UK Government and the Holy See and look forward to renewing this with the visit of Pope Benedict to the UK."

You probably noticed that we changed the four-word idiom to a three word idiom, as we had discussed, and you can see the result. We actually increase the emphasis on the error of judgment by lifting the adjective, instead getting right to the point. What's the phrase? Less is more.

We also strengthen the statement by dropping the words close and productive in describing the relationship between the UK and the Holy See. What is more important is the emphasis placed on the value of the relationship. Point blank; no wasted words; one and out.

A last change returns us to the Law of Thirds in describing the upcoming visit of Pope Benedict. The important and necessary phrases are: looking forward to, renewing and visit. No need for our brains to be bombarded by a second temporal descriptor: later this year. We know it's something in the future. Leave it at that.

An Apple a Day

Enough about government indiscretions. What about corporate America?

Let's talk briefly about Steven Job's Apple Corp. The truth is, the brains behind the iPod and the iPhone nearly made our list of Law of Thirds masters. He was this close, especially given the fact that Apple is built around the concept of the three core business units:

1. Hardware. Their toys are some of the best on the planet. We just named two of them, but we could also mention the iPad, the iTouch, the MacBook and the MacPro
2. Operation Systems. The Mac OS and all its brethren may be competing with mostly free versions of things like Unix, Linux and Android, but it has always been done with a more artistic touch
3. Services. Just drop into an Apple store in your local mall, and you'll know exactly what I mean: wall-to-wall people.

Yes, we could very well be describing Nespresso here, couldn't we? But there are differences.

Yes, most of it works well together, hard to deny that. For example, iTunes, the choice of millions for their listening pleasures, HMV the pure play retailer can't even compete. Microsoft Windows is mostly incompatible with Apple hardware. And Mac OS cannot be installed (legally) on the vast majority of generic hardware. Defensive? You bet! Effective? Indeed.

So where does our Law of Thirds problem lie, you're asking. Let's begin with the size of the organization and the fact that it is fronted by just one man, which for years didn't have a succession plan (though we're assuming there is a pyramid of advisors, yes-men and hobnobbers behind him). We've already seen the problems that Apple can get into when Mr. Jobs isn't around.

In our example about the British Foreign Office, we saw a bunch of people mess up rather badly, and then we saw them mess up even further when it came time to apologize. In the case of Steve Jobs, he found himself apologizing for something he felt (probably justifiably) wasn't actually a problem.

The product in question was the iPhone 4. The issue at hand was a technical one. It turned out that touching the antenna band created reception issues, and people were always touching the antenna band.

Mr. Jobs could have chosen a simple three word idiom to address the problem. We screwed up. Simple, defensive, forgivable. Shrug your shoulders and launch into what Apple intended to do to fix the screw-up.

Nope, not the way he went about it. Instead, he held a press conference with his Chief Operating Office at one arm and his Senior Vice President on the other. Loaded for bear, as the three word saying goes. And what does Mr. Jobs say?

"We screwed up on our algorithm."

Bad move. With the addition of three little words, the sentence evolves from an apology into an enormous hammer that comes down like a ton of bricks on his entire team. Or did he mean a single individual within his organization? No matter. The statement was odd and unnecessary.

First of all, algorithm is such a weak word. In the world of computers, an algorithm is an effective method for solving a problem using a finite sequence of instructions. You could almost hear people shouting, "Come on, Apple, you couldn't even get your algorithm right? What kind of a computer company are you?"

Then, Mr. Jobs decides to call it our algorithm, weakening the statement even further. It makes you think that some guy down in the programming department made up the algorithm all by himself. And if it's your algorithm, then how can you screw it up?

Had the Apple CEO said, "We screwed up the algorithm," the statement all at once becomes broader. It's like they made a bad choice in selecting the algorithm, rather than bungling their own algorithm. It was a collective error. Easier to swallow perhaps, but not much.

Mr. Jobs could also have taken a slightly different approach by just saying, "We're not perfect."

Another powerful three word idiom. Part apology, part explanation, it's just like he's saying, "None of us is perfect," and bringing us all down to the same level. We'd all like to describe ourselves as a little higher up the perfection scale, yet the defensive nature of the idiom means we find it difficult to find a retort. The sentence makes us uncomfortable.

No, I wouldn't mind being at Mr. Jobs' level of creativity and ingenuity, but that's hardly the point.

How does this one sound to you? Phones are not perfect.

If you look at this sentence, we see a complete dearth of thirds. We see an ineffective four-word-statement, or we extrapolate from the sentence and pare it down to a defeatist two-word statement: "not perfect." Another bad move.

During the course of his press conference, Mr. Jobs goes on to compare the iPhone with the competition, wisely or not. He chooses three phones, all with three word names. Does he do this on purpose, or is it just a mental mistake? You be the judge. He cites the HTC Droid Eris, the Blackberry Bold 9700 and the Samsung Omnia II. So instead of confusing his listeners by citing multiple names, or boring them by naming two or less, he stimulates the brain by using the Law of Thirds. Unfortunately, it backfires.

He ends up building a three-legged stool, the ultimate tool for power, stability and reassurance. Then he tries to play it off a weak, insubstantial statement: phones are not perfect.

What happens? The three-legged stool, as it always does, conquers, and his customers flock to the stores looking for the latest, greatest HTC Droid Eris.

What happened next? Mr. Jobs' poorly presented explanation is splashed all over the news, and it comes across as if he is coming down like a ton of bricks on his own team. Shortly thereafter, Mark Papermaster, the Head of iPod and iPhone's Hardware Engineering Division, quits. And while his departure may have not been directly related – it's not for us to say – it is clear that using techniques contrary to the Law of Thirds, in particular when your own team is on the chopping block, is probably more Machiavellian than what Mr. Jobs intended.

An Issue of Economic Proportions

Most of us in the business world have a certain admiration for Dr. Milton Friedman, one of the world's great economists.

That being said, let's look at this single issue quote from the man himself, when he said, "There is one and only one social responsibility of business: to use its resources and to engage in activities designed to increase its profits so long as it stays within the rules of the game, which is to say, engages in open and free competition without deception or fraud."

Heavy stuff indeed, Dr. Friedman (Capitalism and Freedom 1962). But hang on! Isn't this rhetorical? Let's look at it from the point of view of the three appeals: ethical, rational, emotional.

1. Statement one: "...stays within the rules of the game..." Clearly an ethical appeal
2. Statement two: "...use its resources and to engage in activities designed to increase its profits..." Clearly a rational appeal
3. Statement three: "...one and only one social responsibility..." How emotional can you get?

So, the next question is, what point exactly is Dr. Friedman making? Surely, he is essentially coming right out and saying greed is good, though using three lines to wrap the statement in a fluffy coat!

Yes, that was Dr. Friedman doing his best impression of Gordon Gecko, telling all the world's capitalists to run their businesses as a single-issue machine. Disappointing at least on the surface.

But let's not jump to any conclusions. Instead, let's see how a complementary model can increase profits. With that in mind, our first task is to redefine profit. Dr. Friedman was ostensibly referring to shareholder returns when he mentions profits in our quote above, but, in fact, we who advocate the Law of Thirds know that there our three types of returns to consider when talking in such broad strokes. One of the world's great economists should know that, right? They are:

1. Customer return – this refers to the complete and total satisfaction of your customers, whether you are selling to them on a retail or wholesale basis. When your customer experiences positive returns, you've created an effective, great business model. Because if they don't come back, you're out of business!
2. Employee return – we think of employee returns in relation to their salary, and indeed a well-paid employee is more productive than a poorly paid one. But this also refers to benefits, stock opportunities and the rewards of working at a healthy, forward-thinking company
3. Shareholder return – beyond their return on investment, shareholders who are richly rewarded can be relied upon to roll bonds and/or finance new capital-intensive projects.

So, what have we done? We have redefined greed is good according to the Law of Thirds and created an entirely more appealing picture than the one Dr. Friedman was trying to paint.

Having done that, let's now look at the critical interactions that manifest within our new definition. Consider these:

1. Customers to employees: who better to suggest new products and services and to help refine existing business practices than the very customers that a company serves?
2. Employees to customers: who better to educate current customers and potential customers on how best to leverage a company's products than the very employees who sell and represent the products?
3. Employees to shareholders: when employees become shareholders of their company via stock options and the like, this sense of ownership empowers them and naturally enhances their commitment to the success of the business
4. Shareholders to employees: it is in the best interest of the shareholders to have motivated, dedicated employees, and this can be enhanced by bonuses, stock options, and even the underwriting of employee training
5. Shareholders to customers: it behooves shareholders to look at projects and products demanded by the company's customers and to ensure the financing of those with the potential to increase both customer and shareholder returns
6. Customers to shareholders: the best possible scenario is when customers think enough of a company and its products and services to become shareholders themselves; there is nothing like a sense of ownership to motivate people.

Now that we've expanded our view of profit, can we, with all respect, rewrite Dr. Friedman's speech to comply with our expanding view of the Law of Thirds? Well, let's try,

"Business has a responsibility to its customers, employees and shareholders. Profit can be maximized when providing valuable products and/or services via well-trained, motivated and dedicated employees. The by-product is an investor base that is loyal, committed and participatory."

It may not win a Nobel Prize, but it does conform to the Law of Thirds. In this one statement, we see a fair example of the three elements of effective dialogue: balance, predictability and thoughtfulness. Any stakeholder reading such a statement from the CEO of their particular company would feel rightfully reassured.

The Wave Principle

Staring out to breaking waves upon the shore, looking into the flames of a roaring fire, man, or rather the brain's, curiosity to find regulatory, order, repetition, causation, correlation of what he sees rarely ceases. Some of us with an eye to making an extra buck will have studied stock charts, financial statements and market indicators, but not all of us know where it all began. One of the true pioneers in charting stock prices was Ralph Nelson Elliott.

Mr. Elliot was a particularly adept student of the stock market who developed the Wave Principle, a way of identifying trends in various financial markets for investment purposes. Nowadays, these patterns are called Elliot Waves.

Mr. Elliot was also an expert on behavioral economics and how the actions of consumers, borrowers and investors can affect the ebb and flow of stock prices. What Mr. Elliot understood was that when the masses looked at a price history chart, the collective eye would be drawn to a specific point on the chart. The mind naturally interprets that specific point as a signal to either buy or sell, thus causing the price to rise or fall.

Mr. Elliot had all kinds of fancy names for his theories, things like pattern recognition, Fibonacci ratios and golden triangles. People loved it. The get rich crowd lapped it up. Of course, the only person who really made a killing from Mr. Elliot's pearls of pseudo wisdom was his publisher.

The wave principle is based upon a collective investor psychology that moves from optimism to pessimism and back again in a natural sequence. These swings create patterns that Mr. Elliot wanted us to believe could be used to predict price movements. The flaw in this is that he only notes two psychological possibilities: optimism and pessimism.

Another problem. Mr. Elliott's model says that market prices alternate between five waves and three waves at all degrees of a given trend. He says that the dominant trends are noted by waves one, three and five. He calls them 'motive' waves, and each motive wave is also subdivided by five waves. Confused yet? Of course you are. The waves that he ignores, waves two and four, he calls corrective waves. These are the ones that are subdivided in three waves, and these are the ones he wants us to ignore. Sorry, but the Law of Thirds cannot be trumped just because someone puts a fancy name to a theory.

Just like oranges or apples, gold or silver, the price of a stock is just that: the price. A share price has little to do with the price last week or last year. The worth of a stock is simply what the market says it is. As you can imagine, all sorts of things affect the price of oranges and apples. Please don't think stocks are anything different.

That said, it is no surprise that Ralph Nelson Elliot made more money from his books than he did his stock investments. And it's no surprise that even the most time-honored theories cannot buck the logic and the natural thought process of the Law of Thirds. Don't even try.

The Law of Thirds is a powerful thing. It can be used to manipulate, to trick and to fool, just as effectively as we have shown it to be used for gainful purposes. As the corporate motto of Google Inc states, "Don't be Evil".

Epilogue

When we commenced our exploration into the wondrous realm of the Law of Thirds, we asserted and affirmed three indisputable facts about computers:

1. Computers are great at multiplication and addition
2. This book is all about division
3. If there is one thing computers can't do, it's divide.

With that in mind, we also asserted and affirmed three indisputable facts about humans:

1. The human brain, unlike computers, can divide
2. The human brain has a natural propensity to divide things
3. This fact puts us well above computers.

In fact, if computers could divide as well as they multiply and add, then we would have no encryption or online security. What we have instead is a failure turned into a feature; how about that. So there is a need for the human brain after all.

We began our journey by discussing the natural thought processes of the brain, and how, under situations both normal and stressful, competitive and challenging, our brains take information and manage, administer and sort it out to our best advantage. And, we discovered, our best tool in this ongoing intellectual venture proves to be the Law of Thirds.

We continued by exploring the natural flaws inherent in lists and sub-divisions of twos and fours, sixes, eights and tens, and even as high as 24. We found the natural process of our extraordinary brains most often take these lists and sub-divisions and use the Law of Thirds to distil and redefine them.

We then determined that our brains are predisposed to thinking in terms of threes. We said that our brain absorbs information most effectively in thirds. And then we explained how our memories are most effective in remembering when information that is broken down to more manageable and more useful lists and sub-divisions of threes.

We explored a multitude of pertinent examples demonstrating the Law of Thirds in action. We talked about everything from the three-legged stool and three letter acronyms to picture art and the placebo effect. We saw with exceptional clarity how thirds rule the day and make our lives more manageable and more enjoyable.

Like the three basics of every story:

1. Beginning
2. Middle
3. End.

Like the three essentials of every speech:

1. What you say
2. How you say it
3. Who you say it to.

As we saw, every example leads to new levels of understanding and new areas of experimentation.

We started out with communication. We talked about using relationship-based communication rather than direct inferences.

We explored the concept of forming defenses, a most important technique that allows us to function exactly where we are right now. Defend it, and it becomes a better place to be. What's more, people seeking refuge are naturally more attracted to one forming effective defenses. Build a castle and people will be eager to join you, work with you, and bask in the illumination of your sanctuary. Yes, I confess to a bit of purple prose in that last line, but it just seemed to fit.

Finally, we took note of some people and situations that really do exemplify exceptional use of the Law of Thirds and highlighted a couple that, well, exemplify just the opposite. Or, as this priceless three word motto expresses it: live and learn. Or maybe it was a similarly pointed one: everyone is different. How true that is.

So how do you start this process of moving forward, changing, and growing? Benjamin Franklin's most oft-quoted proverb tells us this: "Early to bed, early to rise, makes a man healthy wealthy and wise." But whether you're an early bird or a night owl, focusing on one's own health, wealth and wisdom sounds like a particularly enlightening thing to do, don't you think?

At any rate, not bad for starters. Remember, your brain and mine are happiest when working, playing and processing in sets of three. Whatever the attributes, properties or characteristics, it's pretty much guaranteed that you'll find comfort, contentment, and counsel along the way.

Or as I like to put it, our brains will not be left searching for a 'fourth way.' Sorry, I couldn't resist.

The use of thirds should really be used as a means of turbocharging something. Something you know is important, but, for some reason, something that has fallen behind. Or maybe you're just not exactly sure what that something is, and the Law of Thirds will help identify it. Is there some bad habit that keeps letting you down? Is there a skill you're just not quite proficient with in the workplace, or some strategy or tactic that needs reinforcement in your daily life? Put the Law of Thirds to work, and you'll be pleasantly surprised at the results.

When in doubt, take action by employing the three temporal traits of successful execution:

1. Plan
2. Execute
3. Review.

The combination of these three steps rarely fails. And when they do, pull yourself up by the bootstraps and execute again.

In any case, don't be tempted to review something you had no part in planning. Likewise, don't plan something you are truly incapable of executing. Don't head off on some Quixotic journey when reality is completely against you; yes, it really is too late to learn the electric guitar and start a rock group.

Do you need to persuade other people about the validity of an idea or concept you may want to promote? Present it then by using the Law of Thirds, and they will not only see the idea or concept more clearly, they will be inspired by the presentation.

What about the most mundane of tasks? We all face them day-to-day. At the very simplest of levels, just splitting the task temporarily into a three stage process will make it more important to you, more fun and more doable. Oral hygiene falling behind a bit, has it? Brush, floss, rinse, and your brain will increase the importance level of the task and more care will be taken automatically. Try it for yourself: brush, floss, tongue scrape, gargle, polish, gum massage, you name it. Pick any three, and you'll see yourself perfecting the process in no time.

The power of thirds does that. It's not a theory; it's a fact. Taking a shower? Like most of us, I bet you step in and automatically set the temperature of the water to the level most us call just right. Thinking in thirds, we realized that the other two settings at our disposal are too hot and too cold, but what we forget is that a quick blast of each will boost our circulation, which, I dare say, is a small step to better health, more energy and higher spirits!

Don't go to the gym, for goodness sake. Get outside for exercise, fresh air and something invigorating for your brain. You might just save some membership fees too.

When some unwanted conversationalist makes an unwelcome, even idiotic point, volley right back with an appropriate riposte dedicated to the Law of Thirds, not a terse "indeed" or a cool "exactly". Possibly is boring and truly is truly without merit. Instead, position yourself with a more meaningful three word wonder. You might say, "How dare you?" You might say, "Unlikely at best." Or you might go for the jugular with a more pointed, "Stick it, friend."

It's often said that if knowledge is the route to wealth, then surely all librarians should be rich. But just because you know how to communicate or solve problems in a fashion superior to most others — we're talking the effective use of the Law of Thirds here — it won't automatically make you the next president or the next Warren Buffet.

The ability to read music won't turn you into a musician; I'm sure there are many professional musicians who can't. The ability to write a world-class speech won't turn you into a world-class orator. To best use the Law of Thirds, to maximize its power, and to tap the wonders of your brain's natural thought process, discover first where your talents lie and then magnify them. Pick what you do best and then apply the power of thirds.

Remember in doing so the three makings of a high priority:

1. Things I know not to do
2. Things I must think about
3. Things I must do.

Which leads in turn to the three components in the art of taking action:

1. Decide what needs to be done
2. Do it
3. Review what you did.

In short, take this general rule to heart: whenever you're faced with making a decision, performing a task, or stating a point, split it into three parts. The Law of Thirds simplifies decision-making, gives order to every task and takes a point and gives it emphasis.

You will become more effective in your actions, in your words and in your deeds; people will remember what you did, what you said and how you acted; you will please most of the people most of the time.

So there it is. You have come so far. Your brain is primed.

You really are a practitioner of the Law of Thirds.

Just remember: practice makes perfect!

Or should I say: Yes we can!

www.ingramcontent.com/pod-product-compliance
Lightning Source LLC
Chambersburg PA
CBHW062153080426
42734CB00010B/1671